Pra
DOING BUSINE

Own your table—be a *Viking of Vinifera*—a force in fine food. Command your dinner table and its subjects will endow global domination for dessert. Learn from Tom Black, Old World Master of table techniques on how to transform a meal into a monarchy.

> —JOE BASTIANICH, Preeminent restaurateur, TV personality, author, winemaker, and vineyard owner

If you've ever felt awkward or embarrassed at a business lunch or dinner meeting, you need to read *Doing Business at the Table*. Tom's book will help you effectively handle every imaginable business situation.

> —JEB BLOUNT, CEO of Sales Gravy and author of *Sales EQ*

Which way do you pass the bread? Where does the napkin go? Which wine is best with lobster? Tom's book guides the businessperson through the challenges of doing business at the table.

> —ADAM STRUM, Chairman/CEO Wine Enthusiast Companies, Editor and Publisher *Wine Enthusiast Magazine*

I have had the pleasure of sharing many meals with Tom. Like Tom, I came from humble beginnings and I realized the importance of presenting oneself properly, socially and professionally. *Doing Business at the Table* is full of invaluable information for the salesperson who wants to make a good impression and close the deal, or for someone who wants to competently order wine and food and entertain guests in a restaurant. Tom's book is straightforward, practical, and generous—*just like Tom.*

> —MARTINA MCBRIDE, American country music singer-songwriter and record producer

America has a long history of inviting clients and prospects to lunch and dinner to create relationships and conduct business. In addition to being an entertaining read, Tom's *Doing Business at the Table* is the professional's essential guide on how to organize and preside over a profitable business lunch-dinner meeting.

> —SCOTT CONANT, American celebrity chef, restaurateur, and cookbook author

Tom has made a lifetime effort to learn about food and wine. He shares how to use this extensive knowledge to do business at the table. What makes this book a must is the fact it is a comprehensive read. I literally could not put the book down! As a chef, I have learned so much!

> —DEAN FEARING, Executive Chef/Owner, Fearing's Restaurant, James Beard award winner, and author of *The Texas Food Bible*

DOING
BUSINESS

at the table

TOM BLACK

DOING
BUSINESS

at the table

The GUIDE to presenting an exemplary
professional and social presence while hosting
a successful lunch or dinner business meeting

Requests for permission to reproduce any part of the work should be sent to: info@tomblack.com

Cover design by Revi Ferrer, Ineffable Art
Illustrations by Inese Onckule
Development editor by Nancy Nichols
Interior design by To The Point Solutions
Printing by McNaughton & Gunn
Project Coordinator by Epiphany Imprint Publishing

ISBN: 978-1-7354779-0-9
Library of Congress Control Number: 2020914405

Black, Tom.
Doing business at the table / Tom Black
1. Sales & selling. 2. Meetings & presentations. 3. Business etiquette.
I. Title

Printed in the United States of America

To order additional copies visit: www.tomblack.com

To Bill King,
who started my greatest adventure.

CONTENTS

ACKNOWLEDGMENTS

I would like to express my gratitude to:

Kristin Sullivan, my valuable
Personal Assistant for making my job easier.

Revi Ferrer, an inspiration
and gifted artist; thank you for a brilliant book cover.

Inese Onckule, talented illustrator;
your cartoons rock!

Cathy Lewis, Chef Extraordinaire,
thank you for your guidance through the process.

Nancy Nichols, Development Editor,
thank you for your special touch.

INTRODUCTION

The question is never "who is right?" The question is:
did you establish a business relationship?

—*Tom Black*

*D*oing *Business at the Table* is the American way. Business owners, CEOs, and salespeople entertain their prospects and clients at lunch and dinner meetings to build rapport, present their products and services, and hopefully, close the deal.

Companies are increasingly savvy about their buying decisions. They want a quality product, fair pricing, and they especially want top-notch service. They want to do business with salespeople who are knowledgeable, dependable, accommodating, and efficient. If they cannot get these qualities from you, they will quickly and gladly give their money (your commissions) to your competitor.

Yes, competition is fierce.

I have spent decades developing my social and professional presence so that I would make a favorable impression on a prospect or client. When I was in front of a prospect, I felt like they were judging me, asking themselves was I trustworthy; was I knowledgeable about my products and services; did

I conduct myself in a professional manner. I knew I had to outshine my competition so that my prospects would choose to do business with me over my competitors.

I was hungry for business and financial success. I accepted the instructions (and criticisms) from my bosses and I learned from my mistakes. I attended seminars, I studied my industry, and I honed my product knowledge. I worked hard to improve my leadership, sales, and social skills. My efforts were greatly rewarded. I have enjoyed lifetime as an extremely successful salesperson, business owner, and CEO in the banking industry.

As the CEO of Tom Black Center for Excellence, I have been training and mentoring men and women for over 40 years, helping them cultivate their leadership and sales skills. I wanted to share my knowledge and experiences that have not only made me a multi-millionaire but have gained me nationwide respect and recognition in an ambitious, aggressive banking industry. My career journey motivated me to write *Doing Business at the Table*, a personal growth book for salespeople who seek wealth, professional recognition, and personal achievement.

I cannot tell you how important it is that, as a salesperson, you make a good impression on your prospect or client. Your competition is aggressively pitching your prospects a cheesy smile, a better deal, and mediocre service. But it is not always the cheaper price (or fair pricing) that gets the sale; prospects and clients often award their business to a salesperson with the higher price because they like, respect, and trust a specific salesperson: a man or woman who made a good impression on them because they hosted an impressive lunch or dinner meeting; they presented exemplary professional behavior and proper dining etiquette; they understood food terms and the nuances of wine, and they confidently and proficiently ordered food and wine from the menu at a high-end restaurant. At the conclusion of the salesperson's well-orchestrated lunch or dinner meeting, they presented their products and services with finesse and self-assurance. This salesperson outshined their competition with a polished social and professional presence gaining them the respect and trust of their prospect or client. They formed a meaningful relationship with their prospect. They closed the deal. The prospect became a committed, valuable customer.

If you *truly* want to be a successful and respected salesman or saleswoman, you *must* know how to properly present yourself socially and professionally. You must exhibit dignified behavior in front of your boss, peer group, competition, prospect, or client. You must use proper dining etiquette at a lunch or dinner meeting. You need to have basic knowledge of wine and food on a menu at an upscale restaurant.

Pure and simple—you must outshine your competition if you want to enjoy a lucrative sales career.

My wish for you is that *Doing Business at the Table* helps you make a winning impression on your prospects or clients, build an impressive portfolio of customers, increase your personal income, and ultimately, enjoy a lifetime of personal, business, and financial success.

Now, let's go sell something!

"Do you want to sign the contract before or after dinner?"

THE HISTORY OF
DOING BUSINESS AT THE TABLE

*Food is maybe the only universal thing that really
has the power to bring everyone together.*

—*Guy Fieri*

America has always done business at the table—that is: salespeople use conversation, food, and drink to influence their clients, consummate their deals and exchange billions of dollars.

As a salesperson and CEO, I have spent and approved the spending of millions of dollars on entertaining business prospects and clients. I have often wondered if I were getting a bang for my buck. After reading *Dinner at Mr. Jefferson's* by Charles Cerami, which documented how three men, five great wines and the evening that changed America, I was inspired to share the lessons I have learned at the "salesperson's table."

If you do not know the story of Thomas Jefferson's historical dinner parties, here are the highlights.

George Washington had been in office one year. Thomas Jefferson had returned from France as Secretary of State and Alexander Hamilton was the Secretary of the Treasury. The two men began a feud about the division of power between the central government and the states, thirteen states at the time.

Hamilton wanted a strong federal government. Jefferson and his friend, James Madison, wanted more power to remain with the States. Madison had written most of the constitution and Jefferson had written the Declaration of Independence. Hamilton was offering unique and very liberal ideas that Jefferson and Madison opposed.

President Washington warned all three men that they would cause the failure of the new nation if they did not reach an agreement. At the height of the crisis, Jefferson planned a dinner party for the three men at his home. Having spent the last five years in Paris, he had learned the importance of fine food and wine in business negotiations. Jefferson sought this pleasurable environment to help reach a compromise.

Jefferson carefully thought out his guest list. He invited three men: Alexander Hamilton, James Madison, and himself. He could have invited only Hamilton, or he could have invited more than three guests. He planned the time of arrival at 4:00 p.m. I am sure he wanted to start early so he would have the entire evening to resolve their differences.

Jefferson greeted his guests in the drawing room, and he served a French white wine for this stage of the evening. It was Hermitage, a renowned wine from the northern Rhône wine region of France. Jefferson poured himself only half a glass, a good lesson for all of us at a business dinner. They chatted in the drawing room for half an hour. No business was discussed.

After a friendly discussion with wine, Jefferson took his guests to the dining room, motioning them to be seated at the table. I feel certain he carefully selected their individual seats. The salad course was served; Jefferson served a white wine with this course—a white Bordeaux. We know the vintage was 1786 and the maker Carbonnieux because Jefferson kept immaculate records.

After the salads, the first of two main courses were served—a stuffed capon (young chicken) paired with an Italian red wine from Montepulciano. The second main course was a beef stew served with Chambertin (a red Burgundy). This was a rare and expensive treat in Colonial America.

Before the dessert there were meringues, macaroons, and other sweets treats, and then came the dessert. It was baked Alaska—hot on the outside, cold on the inside. No doubt it made quite an impression on Jefferson's guests. With this final course, Jefferson chose a non-sparkling champagne, most likely sweet, making a memorable impression on his two guests.

Jefferson had set the perfect table of food and wine and only then did the discussion of business begin. The issues on the table were the location of the National Capital and the securing of the National debt by the states to the European powers and banks. During the discussion of these issues, brandy was served. A compromise was reached. The debt was secured, making the dinner "good as gold" and America was able to borrow from the European Banks and nations. The South got the Nation's Capital and the Union survived.

Henry Cabot Lodge said this was "…the single most important agreement before the Civil War." In fact, many historians have said, "…the Union was saved that night."

Interestingly, congressmen, who were reluctant to follow Jefferson's new plan, quietly discussed their plans to alter Jefferson's "compromise" at their own series of dinners.

Could this compromise have been reached in another venue? Or could it have been orchestrated successfully by another hand?

I doubt it.

As entrepreneurs, sales managers, and salespeople we can learn a valuable lesson from Jefferson planning the fine details of a successful dinner meeting.

THE PROBLEM WITH DINNER MEETINGS

After years of watching ineffective meetings conducted at or during meals in restaurants, I decided that a comprehensive guide to doing business at the table would be beneficial to the career salespeople.

John took his best clients out to eat. The restaurant offered high-end steak and a comprehensive wine list—*we have all eaten there.* John made a reservation at the restaurant and then his thought process stopped. After all, it was "just dinner." When they arrived at the restaurant, the reservations were running thirty minutes behind. John and his clients were finally seated at a table by the kitchen where they got an excellent view of every server that passed by and heard every pan and dish rattle in the kitchen. It was the noisiest table in the restaurant.

It developed that one of John's clients did not eat red meat; unfortunately, John did not inquire into his client's food preferences. When the wine list was presented, John, as the host, was asked to order wine. John did not have a clue as to a good wine to order and he did not ask for help. When the wine was presented, it was flawed; John did not recognize it and so it was served. One of his guests did recognize that the wine was flawed and said so. A bit of an embarrassing moment was created, and John's credibility went down another notch.

John had not bothered to arrange the seating at the table and his primary contact sat beside him. No one can talk to someone comfortably when they are seated side by side. John had a difficult time talking to the primary person with whom he was trying to spend the evening.

The steaks came and were overcooked. John did not know what to do and so everyone kept what they were served. The steaks were a disappointment to everyone, and the mood reflected it. More wine and conversation followed, but because John had not planned the flow of the meal, nothing significant was accomplished. The check was presented and again John was bumfuzzled; he did not know whether to tip on the wine or not, so, he left a 2 percent tip. Overall, the sales call and the meal were a bust.

John did what his sales manager asked him to do, he took his important client out to dinner. But did he spend his company's money wisely, and did he further his relationship with his client? Maybe. Was the dinner-sales-call as good as it could have been? No—it was not! That's the problem: Millions of dollars are spent every year by salespeople trying to do business at the table without a clue and without a plan. That dinner could have been a home run for John—*but it wasn't.*

Thomas Jefferson turned over in his grave.

Another salesperson I worked with, Mary, finally got her client to go to dinner. Mary was single and her male client was married. Mary wore a low-cut dress and when the conversation turned personal, she did not know how to handle the situation and she did not want to lose the business or offend her prospect. As the evening progressed, things got worse. No business was accomplished; the future relationship was strained, and Mary never felt comfortable with that prospect again. She spent her company's money and her time poorly. Worse yet, she never got the prospect's business.

Steve took his prospect to dinner. His prospect had never been to a fine dining restaurant, he did not drink and the only item on the menu he recognized was steak. In fact, his prospect asked if he could order a hamburger. It was obvious Steve's prospect felt uncomfortable with the food options and pricy menu. Steve, an experienced diner, was uncomfortable as well, both with his choice of restaurant and his prospect's lack of dining knowledge. Moreover, the prospect probably thought Steve was wasting his company's money, or that Steve's company overcharged their clients to cover expensive business dinners. Did Steve make a sale or advance his relationship with his client? Did he spend his company's money wisely? It's doubtful.

Walt was the CEO of a $100 million-dollar company. His company was for sale and his investment bankers had set up a lunch meeting with a prospective buyer in a private dining room in a New York restaurant. The buyer's entire management team was there. While food was being served, Walt and his investment bankers tried to go through Walt's "book" on the company. The activity in the room was disruptive, making it confusing and difficult to have a business conversation. Walt was an excellent salesman, but he did a poor job presenting the potential of his company because he and the investment bankers could not control the atmosphere. The prospective buyers were never heard from again. *However*, it was a great lunch!

Remember: a meeting with a customer or prospect over a meal is not a social event—it is a business meeting and sales call— pure and simple.

CHAPTER 1

SETTING GOALS:
PREPARING FOR A MEETING

The journey of a thousand miles
begins with but a single step.

—*Lao Tzu*

"This agreement doesn't obligate you to anything and we will do anything you want."

J efferson understood that to have a successful meeting, goals must be established for what is to be accomplished at that meeting. We as entrepreneurs, sales managers and salespeople should do the same.

Before a meeting with your client or prospect, ask yourself: What do you want to accomplish? Is your goal to:

1. Create a shared experience and build a better relationship?

2. Understand your prospects'/clients' business better?

3. Identify needs for your products and services?

4. Sell your product or service?

5. Solve existing problems?

6. Solve potential problems?

7. Introduce a new company associate?

8. Transfer an account to another associate?

9. Say "thank you" for your customer's business?

10. Establish equal footing with your client outside of their office, where they have less control of the situation?

You are probably going to spend $200 to several thousand dollars on a nice dinner for prospects or clients. You should take it seriously when you invest your time and your company's money. You should tell yourself, *my time is valuable. If I spend "x" I should get this return. I want to make my time count.*

Your goals should be written down, they should have a time frame, and when your goals are set, they should be communicated to someone who is important to your success. Your dinner or lunch goals should be what you intend to accomplish in a short time frame—not long-term. Short time frames make it easier for you to accomplish your goals.

Before the meeting, communicate your goals to your associates who are attending the meeting. If more than one person from your company is involved in a business meeting, then a full discussion of the goals is in order, as well as a discussion of roles for each participant.

Your prospect or client should also be aware of the meeting agenda. You should communicate as much about your goals as possible; it will set the tone for your lunch or dinner meeting and define your expectations.

I have seen many dinners where the prospect or client was surprised by the agenda; nothing positive was achieved in this scenario.

Remember: Success by the inch is a cinch, by the yard it's hard.

SET THE APPOINTMENT

If your intention is to sell something, then mentioning the "intention to sell" is appropriate and necessary. For example: "Bill, one thing I'd like to discuss at dinner is our strategy for implementing our product, program, etc." Your intention is best communicated before the meeting.

Many times, I have left lunch and dinner meetings disappointed because nothing was accomplished. The purpose of the meeting was unknown during the dinner (even to the salesperson). After the meeting, the salesperson said to me, "I thought that went well," when in fact, nothing was accomplished except eating a meal for which we paid the tab. The objective of these meetings was not thought out, not planned, and consequently, the salesperson was not prepared. When these dinners or lunches did go well—*it was largely by accident.*

Sometimes a blind hog can root an acorn now and then.

Once the meeting is set, and the purpose for a dinner has been communicated to the prospect or client, it is a good idea to confirm the dinner meeting in writing. E-mail the client with the details: the date, time, and place, and if appropriate include a personal note like, "I'm looking forward to seeing you and discussing our program." This confirms the dinner, lets the prospect or client know that you are looking forward to your time together, and that there is a business element to the dinner. Sales managers, CEOs and anyone with budget responsibility should make this a rule.

You have set the appointment with your prospect or client and you have confirmed it in writing. Now, the work and the fun begin!

CHAPTER 2

SELECTING A SUITABLE RESTAURANT FOR A MEETING

The restaurant where you choose to take your prospect or client is fully forty percent of the success of the meal and the meeting.

"The lowest calorie offering is the celery stalk."

Picking the restaurant is not about you; it is to please the prospect or client and gain his respect, trust, and business.

I was born in a boxcar with an outside bathroom. I knew absolutely nothing about entertaining a prospect or client in a nice restaurant, but that did not stop me from inviting them to lunch or dinner. I soon noticed that when my prospect or client and I engaged in a conversation at a meeting, and especially when I was sitting with my prospect or client at lunch or dinner, they were judging everything I did, as if they were looking for a reason to do business with me—*or not*. I knew I had to up my game to get their business. I learned about wine, how to understand an upscale restaurant menu, and how to use proper dining manners to make a good impression on my clients.

In the following pages, I write about my journey from living in a boxcar, to acquiring in-depth wine knowledge and social and business etiquette, honing my sales skills, and ultimately dining in the greatest restaurants in the world.

More importantly, this personal growth process has allowed me to make millions of dollars.

Here are some tips to help you choose the suitable restaurant for hosting a business dinner or lunch:

1. **Location**—Nothing is worse than being late or causing your prospect or client to be late because of a restaurant's obscure location and difficult parking. When choosing a restaurant ask yourself: Is the restaurant close to the prospect's or client's place of work? Is the location easy to find? Is there convenient parking or valet? Is the parking lot easy for both you and your prospect to get in and out of? GPS has made finding restaurants easier, but I cannot tell you how many times a restaurant that was difficult to find has set the wrong tone for the lunch or dinner meeting.

   Mike picked a new, trendy restaurant for lunch. It was so new his prospect could not find it in any digital map. The prospect was late to the restaurant and they were understandably frustrated and embarrassed. Lunch was served, we had to eat hurriedly, and no business was accomplished. Mike's restaurant was a bad decision.

   I attended a lunch meeting as the CEO of our company. My prospect arrived at the restaurant 30 minutes late. It was raining; the prospect was soaking wet, complaining that he could not find a parking place. This does not help to create a buying atmosphere. I am sure the prospect thought my company was the one who was all wet for picking that restaurant location.

2. **Dress**—Make sure the dress code is communicated. If you are meeting directly after work, work clothes are appropriate. Keep in mind that the prospect's or client's workplace dress code could be khakis and a golf shirt or a suit and tie. Bottomline: dress like your prospect or client and everyone will be more comfortable.

   Years ago, I went to dinner with a bank prospect. He wore a suit; I was in shirt sleeves. I was uncomfortable the whole evening and I think my prospect was too. It never happened again. I think we have all experienced a clothing mistake in a business or social setting. My thought is: It is always better to over dress than to under dress. If you arrive at an after-hours business meeting over dressed, a man can always take off his tie; a woman can downplay her accessories.

3. **Menu**—Unless you know your prospect's likes and dislikes, you need to get his approval on your restaurant selection. Say something like, "I thought we'd go to ABC—would that work for you?" It also does not hurt to ask about your prospect's dietary restrictions. I have invited vegans to inappropriate restaurants because I did not ask.

   Dale loved big steak restaurants and he frequented the same steak places. This was good for him, but it was awkward when he took a non-red meat eater to lunch. The prospect was nice about his dislike of red meat, but Dale never sold him anything. Was that the reason for a no sale? Maybe. Maybe not. But I feel it did not help Dale's efforts. Keep in mind, prospects and clients ask themselves, *Do I want to do business with you?*

4. **Reservations**—It is best to select a restaurant that takes lunch and dinner reservations. When you have a reservation, expect the restaurant to honor it, seating you at the agreed-upon time. Nothing is worse than having a hungry or impatient prospect or client who must wait to be seated at a table. This will not work for a business dinner.

If you get to a restaurant and the reservations are running behind, you can usually move up on the list by speaking to the manager. Try something like, "Chris (manager), we have to catch a flight, be home to relieve the babysitter at 9:00, etc. Can we be seated as soon as possible?"

I was part-owner of a restaurant in New York—they were always busy. One night a familiar customer came in with three clients; he did not have a reservation and every table was full. Patrick, the restaurant manager, did not tell the customer he was not in the book, he instead, said, "One moment" and the staff quickly set up a table on the landing to the second floor where no one had ever sat before. The four men were seated in ten minutes.

If you do not have a reservation, great restaurants will find a way to accommodate you. If they don't, never go back and warn your friends too.

Babbo was the hardest reservation in New York City. However, I can call the day I want to dine and there is always a table for me. *Why?* I developed a relationship with the maître d'. You can too; it just takes a little extra effort. Call the maître d' by his name, shake hands with him, ask about his family, business, etc.

You will stand out in his mind because most people won't or don't take the time to express their appreciation to the restaurant staff.

Most restaurants want you to be happy, but they hate rude people. You are a salesperson—act like one and be pleasantly persistent and you will recoup rewards beyond your imagination.

Like my friend, James Wedgeworth says, "S.E.E.D.S." Sometimes Extra Effort Determines Success.

5. **Time Frame**—When planning a business lunch or dinner, you need to consider how long you want the meal to last. Obviously, the longer the meal the more time you will have to accomplish your goals. However, you must consider your prospect's feelings and pick a restaurant that fits his time frame as well.

    I have found that earlier dinners work best for me and I usually suggest 6:00 p.m. so that the prospect can come straight from work. If this is not convenient, they will let you know, and you can move your reservation to a later time.

    An earlier dinner helps to get my prospect home at a decent hour. Nothing is worse than keeping your prospect or client from his or her family when being at home is preferred. Equally bad is a lunch that is too long and gets your guest back to work late. When I make an appointment for lunch, I ask my prospect or client, "Do you need to be back by 1:00 or 12:30 or 1:30?" and I then plan our time together accordingly.

6. **Atmosphere**— Here, I see a lot of mistakes. The restaurant menu and service could be the best you could imagine, but if they do not have great atmosphere in which to do business—*don't go to this restaurant*. One time I went to a business lunch meeting where the host chose a Mexican restaurant with a table outside in the sun. *Boy, did we get hot.* I like to sit outside as well as the next guy, but I never have a lunch or dinner meeting outside. Too many uncontrollable things can occur outside: the temperature can be too hot or cold; there can be bugs in the food, water, or wine; the wind can be blowing, other things can go wrong as well. One salesperson said that one time when he was dining outside, a bird pooped on his head! These are things you just cannot overcome.

The restaurant atmosphere must be quiet. I love a busy restaurant, but distractions are just that—distractions—and I want a captive audience when I am talking to a prospect. Look for restaurants that have private areas. On occasions, I have asked for a private room if the group is large enough and the topic of discussion needs privacy. Lighting is also critical. Dark restaurants are not conducive for looking at business proposals, nor does a dimly lit room create a business atmosphere. I know I am spoiling your fun, but remember, the most fun is making the sale!

If you are at a table in the general population of the restaurant, then table selection is especially important. Years ago, I had dinner with my boss and a group of prospects. We were seated at a table next to the kitchen. All night long, we heard the banging and clanging of pots, pans, and dishes. Truly little business was done, but I did learn a valuable lesson. Tables by the kitchen or front door can be noisy and disruptive to your conversations, while a table in a corner can minimize the surrounding activity. Your table must have enough privacy that you can carry on a discussion.

When you make your reservation select a table with the desired privacy and request it; you may have to be persistent and a little demanding to get your desired table. If you cannot get a specific table guaranteed, then I suggest you go to another restaurant. Keep in mind, you are spending your or the company's money to accomplish certain goals. Do not settle for less than your best or the best table in the restaurant.

An investment banker recently took me to a popular restaurant to discuss with him selling a company I owned. The banker arrived late to our meeting, he left early, his table was a round eight-top (an unbefitting table for two people having a sensitive business conversation) and the super-sized table was in the middle of a busy, noisy restaurant. We spent the evening saying, *"What?"* to each other. Terrible planning! If you want to have a successful business meeting, select a restaurant that works for you, not one that is popular and noisy.

As far as restaurant atmosphere is concerned, to avoid an unsuitable business environment, go where you have been before. Salespeople frequently say, "In selling, we get pre-approach information about a prospect before we make the sales call." The same goes for the restaurant atmosphere. You should know what a restaurant is like (menu, seating, service, and atmosphere) before you take a client there. If you plan to have a business meeting at a new restaurant, you need to make a pre-visit. It makes sense to avoid surprises.

7. **Budget**—My ex-wife had an unlimited budget and she exceeded it. It is my opinion that moderation in all things is good—even when it comes to moderation. If your company does not have a recommended expense policy, establish one yourself.

   If the restaurant is expensive, your prospect may think this company makes too much money or that a salesperson is irresponsible with his company's money. Either sentiment is not to your benefit. By the same token, if you take your client to McDonald's, you will not make a great impression. If it is a first lunch or dinner with a prospect or client, choose a moderately-priced restaurant with good food and your prospect cannot be critical of you. If it is an established client relationship, you should know the client's restaurant preference.

8. **Ethnic Restaurants**—Most people enjoy a new and exciting dining experience. Mexican, Greek, Thai, Chinese, and Indian restaurants offer traditional cuisines that can please a person's palate but can also present dining problems when entertaining a potential client. Unless specifically requested by a prospect or client, I try to stay with traditional

American restaurants. Italian is an exception, as most Italian restaurants have a forgiving menu.

I will never forget the time Mark, our salesperson, took his prospect to a traditional Japanese restaurant. Mark was comfortable using the chopsticks. His prospect and I used a fork and knife. Mark's prospect was intimidated by the menu; he didn't know sushi from tempura. Mark, acting as our Japanese food guide, had a great time; his prospect's experience, however, could have been better.

The same goes for a high-end restaurant. I have been with salespeople who took the prospect to a fancy new restaurant where no one was familiar with the menu items. I felt uncomfortable and I am sure everyone else did as well. In fact, the prospects made fun of the menu; what was supposed to be a treat by the salesperson, became a joke. This was not a positive experience.

While new dining experiences are fun and interesting among friends and colleagues, a trendy restaurant may not be appreciated in a new business relationship. If I am trying to make a good impression and build a relationship on common interests, I try to pick a restaurant where everyone will find something on the menu they like. I avoid spicy foods that will get someone in trouble and raw fish that may put someone in a bad mood. I am especially careful about selecting a restaurant for large group dinners where someone might object to food that is not mainstream.

My advice: Don't risk making your prospect uncomfortable with your choice of an ethnic or high-end restaurant.

CHAPTER 3

MEETING YOUR CLIENT AT THE RESTAURANT

To invite a person to dinner is to place them under observation. Every dining room is a temporary prison where politeness chains the guest to the table.

—*Maurice Renard,* The Hands of Orlac

The day of the lunch or dinner meeting arrives, and everyone makes it to the restaurant with no hitches. You greet each other in the lobby and exchange introductions, and as the host, you check in at the host-hostess stand.

I have had times when my reservation has not been honored or it has been lost. Worse yet, the person making the reservation for me forgot to call the restaurant to make the reservation. If this happens, you will feel embarrassed, but you will get through it.

Find the manager, take him aside, explain your situation and ask for his help. Your sincere explanation will go far with the manager; many times, I try to tip him as well. If this doesn't work—*you're stuck*. Do not leave to go to another restaurant unless it is next door and a table is immediately available, because you will waste more time. Make your group or individual as comfortable as possible; wait patiently for a table and use the wait-time to build a relationship with your prospect or client.

I will never forget the time I was having dinner with a banker prospect whom I had been trying to sell for over a year. I had a good relationship with him, and it was just the two of us for dinner. We waited an hour for our table and while waiting, my prospect got pretty drunk. When we got to the table he was blasted, and although our relationship improved, we did no business. These things can happen, but in a sales situation, we will lose the sale. All you can do is try to be as prepared as possible.

BEING SEATED AT THE TABLE

The maître d' or hostess takes you to the table; hopefully, you have given some thought to how you want people to sit. You should always be facing your prospect across the table, never sitting beside him or down the table too far away. I like to sit facing the wall, so I am not distracted; nothing is worse than a salesperson who is looking around at everyone and everything going on in the restaurant.

Everyone is seated and the menus are presented. This should not be the first time you see this restaurant menu because you perused their menu online, or you have eaten there before, or you stopped by earlier to check it out. Sometimes there will be terms on the menu you do not recognize. That is a good reason to look up words on the menu you do not understand before you get to the restaurant. Imagine how impressed your guests will be when you are the only one at the table who can explain the cuts of meat and preparation terms on a high-end menu. It may seem like a small thing, but it builds confidence in your abilities and it makes you more attractive as a business partner or vendor. The point is: there should be no surprises in a business setting.

The prospect orders first. If women are present, the women order first and, as the host, you order last.

Pay attention to what your prospect orders; you can make your prospect feel comfortable by following their lead. If your prospect orders three courses, you order three courses. If they order one course, you order one course. If they ask to share, you share. If they pass on dessert, you pass on dessert. If they order dessert, you order dessert, even if you only take one bite. Making the sale comes first; eating and food are secondary.

I cannot say enough about the intangible of "wanting to do business with you."

People like to do business with people who seem like themselves. I typically find an instant connection with someone who shares my passion for fine wine. It is the same with food. We enjoy dining with friends who enjoy the same restaurants.

Make your prospect want to do business with you by mirroring them. If your prospect orders a salad and you order two courses—you will seem different from them. They may even apologize for not being hungry or trying to lose weight. If you want to build a connection with your client, to some extent, mimic what he or she orders. If your client orders a salad, you should eat a salad. Your client will feel validated in his or her selection of food, putting them at ease. If you are still hungry when you leave the restaurant, stop somewhere to get a burger. Likewise, if your prospect or client orders two courses and you only order a salad—you will seem different from them. If your client orders two courses, you should order two courses. There are no food police; if you cannot eat two courses, take one bite of each and then ask for a doggie bag (apologize to your guests for your unrefined manners) and discreetly take the leftovers home to your German Shepard. The lunch or dinner is about building a relationship—not about your diet or lack of one.

Many times, the waiter will offer you water: ice water, still, or sparkling. Defer to your guests. Do not be the only one who orders bottled water; it looks pretentious and spends your company's money unnecessarily. If your guests want bottled water, then that's fine. It is a poor pun, but "go with the flow" on this one.

CHAPTER 4

MAKING PROPER INTRODUCTIONS

Be so good they can't ignore you.

—*Steve Martin*

I f you or your guests do not know everyone at the lunch or dinner, as the host it is your job to introduce the attendees, making everyone feel at ease and create a harmonious environment.

Here are a few rules for making effective introductions.

- If you are seated, stand up. Nothing is worse than a lazy, seated introduction which can make a bad impression to your guests. Standing up shows respect and makes you appear in your best light.

- I hate it when I cannot understand someone's name, or I do not know who they are in the organization. If you know their name, use it. If you do not know their name, get it. If you do not hear their name correctly, ask, "Can you repeat that?" or "Can you spell that?"

- Handshakes should be done web to web. I am not talking Spiderman, but thumb web to thumb web— never fingertip to fingertip. Stand up straight, look the person in the eye, and smile. Your handshake should be firm but not overly aggressive. Never give them a limp fish. When you shake hands, say, "Nice to meet you."

- Say everyone's name correctly and clearly. As the host, you can also offer a person's position in the company so that everyone is informed. A one sentence explanation of who they are is acceptable, for example, "Bill is the head of our operations team." Do not give a speech.

- If you have forgotten a name you should know, or you struggle to remember last names, here is a trick that usually works. "I am going to let you introduce yourselves today." If I can't remember last names, I use everyone's first name; people will tell each other their last names anyway. However, these are fallbacks— the professional salesperson acquires everyone's name prior to a meeting. Many times, I will write names down on a 3x5 card and put it in my pocket, sometimes writing the name phonetically so I can get the pronunciation right. Better safe than sorry.

One night I was at a dinner meeting with a salesperson and their prospect. The salesperson introduced me to the prospect. I thought his name was Herb. I called him Herb for thirty minutes before he told me his name was Irv. If I had taken the time to inquire about the prospect's name before the meeting, I would not have called him by the wrong name. I could hear Irv telling his co-workers the next day, "What a jerk. He called me Herb for half the evening." I was mentally lazy, and I got burned.

- There is a protocol about using first names. If you are 15 years younger than the person you are introducing, use "Mr. Johnson," not "Jim Johnson." You may use first names if you have their permission, or if everyone else calls someone by their first name. From a sales point of view, it is better to use first names because that is how we talk to our friends. If you are in your 50s, you can use first names for everybody. You should introduce the person with the most authority first. If you are not sure, then start with the eldest. You should know what order to introduce everyone before you get to the meeting.

- The introductions have been made and now the fun can begin. If the fun does not begin, it is your job to get it started. Once you have the conversation going, you can excuse yourself or just be a good listener. However, if the meeting is dull or boring or unproductive, that is your fault.

- As the host, it is your job to stimulate the conversation. I teach two easy techniques. First, have a series of pre-planned questions. Remember, people will talk about themselves and things they are interested in. Here are some questions you can use:
  - How was your day?
  - What is your hometown?

- Where did you go to school?
- Did you play sports in school?
- Are you a sports fan?
- Do you have children?
- Do you have any hobbies?
- Have you been on any trips lately?

If you do not like these questions, create your own.

The second technique is to develop an interesting, entertaining story. The true story I sometimes tell is:

> *I lived with my family in a railroad boxcar that was divided into two bedrooms with one tiny living space and an outdoor bathroom. I never realized I was poor until, in the seventh grade, kids at school made fun of my clothing. This was a turning point for me. It motivated me to become a successful, wealthy businessman.*
>
> *"Really?" people ask.*
>
> *"Yes," I say, "I wrote the book* Boxcar Millionaire.*"*

People love stories of overcoming adversity, funny tales about pets, brief narratives of exceptional vacations, research and statistics, or an amusing tell-all story about yourself. I cannot give you a story, you must create your own and then practice telling your story to your friends, co-workers, spouse, etc. Get them to tell you if, in fact, your story is entertaining and interesting because nothing is worse than a lengthy, boring story.

The point is: use stories to entertain and help form relationships with your guests.

I have included "Tips for Good Business Conversation" later in the book.

CHAPTER 5

APPROPRIATE (AND INAPPROPRIATE) BUSINESS BEHAVIOR

---

*Filter everything you're doing, saying
and pitching through the customer point of view,
and you'll improve just about every metric
you care about today.*

—*Matt Heinz*

Salespeople are made, not born, or so the saying goes. Some personalities are a natural fit for the sales profession; they have an innate ability to listen, are enthusiastic and empathetic, and have good manners that gain a prospect's or client's respect and help the salesperson close the sale. Others seeking a sales career may need to develop the qualities of top sales performers. Here are my top behavioral tips that can help you make the sale or kill the deal. Many of these tips have come from great salespeople like John Chapin.

1. If a prospect or client tells you that you are not going to get their business, smile, find out the reason, and thank the person for his or her time. If you appear disgruntled that you lost the sale, your client may regard you as unprofessional. If you continue to try to sell your client, he will think you are an obnoxious, pushy salesperson. Remain amicable toward your client, sincerely thank them for their time, respectfully tell them that you still want their business, and then exit courteously. He or she will remember you favorably, and you have left the door open for a future sales opportunity.

2. If your client is traveling with you and your business associate in your car, always offer the front passenger seat to the client. It shows respect. If a client insists on sitting in back seat, you can let them.

3. When dining, do not sit down until the customer or prospect is seated first at the table; this is a gesture of respect. Ask your server his or her name and use it to address them. Never say, "Hey you." While eating, if your plate has more food on it than the other person, *you are talking too much*. When the meal has ended, if your guest glances at their watch or iPhone—order the check immediately. Always pick up the check; it says you are confident and in control; qualities that make you a desirable business partner.

4. Selling is a profession in which the salesperson is selling themself; he or she attempts to develop a relationship with the prospect or client, and hopefully sell their product. Do not be overly competitive, and if possible, sometimes let the customer win when negotiating a deal. Make sure you have honed your sales skills before you try to bond with a customer during the selling conversation.

5. People watch you and judge you by the way you treat others. Extend common courtesy to everyone you encounter; be friendly and polite to the receptionist in your client's front office, the parking lot attendant, and the restaurant waitstaff; be pleasant to the people you pass on the street, and especially be courteous to your competition. It takes a half a minute to smile, say hello, have a nice day, and thank you. Help a woman on and off with her coat; help her with her coat before you take off or put on your coat. If she has

a neck scarf, tuck it halfway into the sleeve. This can take some practice.

6. Never assume anything and keep an open mind about everything. An open mind creates many surprise opportunities.

7. People like to do business with people who are uplifting and positive-minded. If you whine about something (the food, service, or atmosphere) you will look like someone who has a negative outlook on life; someone who is hard to get along with. This makes you less attractive as a business partner.

8. Watch what you say, never say anything you do not want someone to hear or repeat. For the most part, avoid controversial topics: politics, religion, personal finances, and intimate conversations about health, family, and relationship issues. These are inappropriate conversation topics with a prospect or client.

9. Put your phone away. Answering a call or even glancing at your phone in the presence of a prospect or client is the epitome of rude behavior. Do not leave your phone face down on the dining table; it looks like you are waiting for a call. Turn the ringer off and leave it in your pocket or purse or leave it in your car. If you must take an urgent call, excuse yourself and step outside the room.

10. Do not gossip. People do not trust someone who gossips. They know if a person talks about someone behind their back, they will eventually bad-mouth you as well. Gossip makes you look untrustworthy and insecure.

11. Do not drink too much. If your client wants to get hammered at dinner, that is his hangover. As a salesperson, your job is to stay sober, stay focused, and appear professional. If you get even a little tipsy, your client will lose respect for you and not trust you and you will permanently lose his business.

12. Do not use foul language around clients or in the workplace. Some jokes and expressions just seem to have more impact with a bawdy four-letter word. One crude word can offend a prospect or client and cost you a sale. Save your off-color language for when you are drinking wine with your friends.

13. Always give the customer or prospect a chance to save face. If your client says something that is obviously wrong, you do not have to correct them. Challenging a client can cause them to lose face, and consequently, cost you the sale. The sale is more important than who is right.

14. Know your prospect's or client's name prior to the meeting. Inquire in advance as to the prospect's full name, title, and position within his company; when you meet, pronounce the client's name correctly and confidently.

15. When presenting a gift, brochures, or proposals to a client, make sure all items are clean, (not wrinkled or soiled) and written information is concise and professional in appearance. A polished presentation tells a prospect or client you are conscientious and organized.

16. Carry a high-quality ink pen and make sure that the pen works. By high quality, I mean something

that looks good—not a cheap Bic Clic pen. Your pen should have black or blue ink, unless you have a reason related to your business that dictates another color. Carry a backup pen in case your pen suddenly runs out of ink in the middle of your client signing your $10 million contract. If you exchange business cards, *never* give out more than one card.

17. The car you drive projects a certain image. You can impress people with a nice car. You can turn people off with a clunker. You can make people jealous with an expensive car. If you drive a Mercedes, a potential customer may decide you make too much money. If you drive a car with a dented fender, a client may think you do not take care your possessions. If your car is dirty and littered with trash, a client may think you are lazy and inefficient. When selecting a car, your objective is to drive a business car that is appropriate for what you are selling and one that puts you in a position in which you are least likely to be judged negatively. If you have a company car, you can disregard this advice.

18. Send a follow-up email within 24 hours after a meeting. Make it short and to the point, thank your client for their time and hopefully for the sale. If you did not make the sale, reiterate the purpose of the meeting, and ask for a follow-up conversation or meeting.

Remember: Proper business behavior tells the prospect or client that you are respectful, efficient, and dependable; qualities that will help you gain the prospect's or client's trust and close the sale.

CHAPTER 6

DO'S AND DON'TS AT
THE DINING TABLE

The world was my oyster,
but I used the wrong fork.

—Oscar Wilde

Table Setting

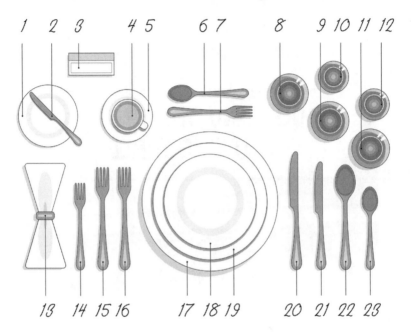

1 Bread Plate

2 Butter Knife

3 Place Card

4 Coffee Cup

5 Coffee Saucer

6 Dessert Spoon

7 Dessert Fork

8 Water Goblet

9 Red Wine Glass

10 Champagne Flute

11 White Wine Glass

12 Sherry Glass

13 Napkin

14 Salad Fork

15 Fish Fork

16 Dinner Fork

17 Dinner Plate

18 Soup Bowl

19 Salad Plate

20 Dinner Knife

21 Salad Knife

22 Dinner Spoon

23 Soup Spoon

I t is time to notice the table setting: the plates, glasses, forks, knives, and spoons. These are your weapons that can enhance your dining experience or be your culinary downfall. Here are some general rules about place settings and the importance of dining do's and don'ts.

1. Flatware is placed in order of use. Start on the outside of the place setting and work your way inward toward the plate. Forks go on the left, with the salad fork first, and then the dinner fork beside the plate. On the right side of the plate, you will find the knife, appetizer or salad knife, spoon, soup spoon, and oyster fork. Knives, forks, and spoons laid horizontally at the top of your charger or plate are for dessert; do not use these until it is time for dessert.

2. In general, a fork always has a corresponding knife. A cocktail fork is the exception.

3. Glassware goes above the knife and spoon on the right. Basic glassware is the water goblet, champagne flute,

red wine glass, white or rose wine glass, the sherry, port, Sauterne glass, coffee cup and teacup. The waiter will provide the proper wine glass for your selection of wine. Which glasses are yours? The ones on your right.

4. If there is a plate already on the table when you sit down, this is a "charger." Charger plates, also called a "service plate," are used to dress up the dinner table. Do not eat from this plate or put food on it.

5. If there is a small plate to the left of your charger or dinner plate, this is your bread plate, salad plate, or vegetable plate. Sometimes there will be a butter knife or butter spreader. This should always be placed across the top of the bread plate; it should never be on the tablecloth or table. If there is no bread plate, use your dinner plate; bread never goes on the table. Which bread plate is yours? The one on your left.

6. Pass the breadbasket to the right. Let people get their own bread; do not hand them bread with your fingers. Do not start eating your bread before your food arrives. Do not play with the bread and do not tear the crust off and eat only the soft middle. Do not spread pâté on your bread; eat them separately. Put the pâté in your mouth with your fork and then take a bite of bread. Do not mop up the sauce with your bread. I have done it—*but then I was born in a boxcar*! If your host mops up the sauce, put a small piece of bread on the end of your fork and sop up the sauce.

7. Bread is to be broken into small pieces and one piece eaten at a time. Butter is spread on the small pieces, not the whole roll. Bread and butter are both passed

to the right (counterclockwise). If there is no butter knife, then use your dinner knife (remember you may have more than one knife). If that is the case, when you finish with the dinner knife, place it on the top of your dinner plate as it is too large to place on the bread plate.

8. Serving sliced bread is preferable; do not put an unsliced loaf of bread on the table and expect your guests to slice it. If the bread is not sliced, only slice it for yourself.

The use of the napkin began in Reims, France in the Court of Charles VII. Before the early 15th Century, napkins were used only by Kings and Princes and they were always trimmed in lace. Today there are over 400 ways to fold a napkin.

9. Somewhere on the table will be your napkin. Some restaurants will have the waiter place the napkins for everyone in their lap; other restaurants only place the ladies' napkins, while other restaurants let each guest place their own napkin. (Watch what is happening around you and you will know what to do.) If the waiter does not assist with your napkin, put your napkin on your lap as soon as you sit down; unfold it halfway with the fold facing the waistline. When you

leave the table, your napkin goes on the chair, not the table. Never place your napkin on the table until dinner is over.

10. Do not turn your wine glass or coffee cup upside down to denote the fact that you do not want the beverage. If you do not want wine or coffee, cover the glass with your hand when the server offers the beverage.

11. Never hold your wine glass by the bowl; hold it by the stem. Holding the wine glass by the bowl will warm up the wine and leave fingerprints on the glass. If it is a stemless wine glass (which in my opinion is in bad form), grab the glass at the base instead of holding it at the top or middle.

12. Salt and pepper should always be passed together, even if someone asks for just the salt. Set them both on the table near the person who asked for them, not in their hands. Aside from general good manners, some people believe it is bad luck to pass salt from one hand to another person's hand or to pass them separately.

13. Cut one bite of food at a time: the smaller the bite, the better. Small bites are easier to chew and faster

to swallow so a mouthful of food does not interfere with your conversation. Best of all, small bites make you less likely to choke. I have often seen people cut up two or more bites of food at a time. Your food gets cold faster and it is not good manners. The exception is: if you are cutting up food for a child or you are helping someone with their food.

14. No elbows on the table. It reflects bad posture and people with bad posture are perceived as having low energy and not interesting to talk to. People are hesitant to do business with people who hunch over at the table—*you don't want that*! During the meal, you may rest your wrists on the edge of the table—*but only your wrists*! However, when food is not present or the table is being used as a desk, you may put your elbows on the table.

15. No medicine at the table. If you must take a pill or other medicine, or use a toothpick to clean your teeth, leave the table and come back. My dad always had a toothpick in his mouth. I thought nothing of it. I still remember my boss saying to me, "Are you going to make me watch you pick your teeth." Never again. Even if you cover your mouth, picking your teeth is always done in private.

All grooming at the table is inappropriate; do not apply lipstick, comb your hair, or look in your compact mirror. These are best done in the restroom. Saleswomen have said to me, "What's the difference?" My response, "If one person thinks less of you because you do it, *then why do it*?" It is ill-mannered to take medicine or groom yourself at the table, and it is inconsiderate and offensive for a man or woman to wear too much cologne or perfume. People will judge you based on your manners—why risk it?

16. When you take a break from eating your meal, your silverware never goes back on the table, it is always placed on your plate. If you have not finished eating, place your silverware at four o'clock and seven o'clock (where four and seven would be on a clock face) with the fork tines up on your plate. This is a common signal to the server that you are *not* finished eating. When you have finished eating, place both fork and knife on your plate at the four o'clock position, the blade of your knife should face inward; the fork tines may be either up or down. This signals to the server that you have finished eating. Additionally, food is served from the left and plates are cleared from the right; it is a convenience to the server to remove your plate with the utensils on the right.

17. Cutting your meat may seem simple, but I have seen highly paid executives violate this simple process. Pick up the fork with your left hand and then pick up the knife in your right hand and cut your meat or other dish (one piece at a time), and then place the knife across the back of the plate with the blade facing down. Next, stab your food with your fork or slip your fork under your food, take a bite, and put your fork down on the plate. Repeat this process for all meat, one bite at a time.

Note: The American style of eating is with the fork in the left hand and the knife in the right hand when cutting food; place the knife in resting position on

Utensil Etiquette

Start

Pause

Ready for 2nd plate

Finished

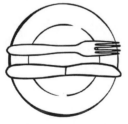

Excellent

Do Not Like

your plate and use the fork in your right hand to bring the food to your mouth with the fork prongs facing upward. The Continental (or European) style of eating is with the fork held in the left hand (for eating) and the knife in the right hand (for cutting), bringing your food to your mouth with your left hand with the fork prongs facing downward. The fork and knife remain in the left and right hands throughout the meal, laying your silverware down in its resting position when you need to take a drink or eat bread. When done correctly, either is acceptable.

18. Do not use your fingers (unbelievably, some people do this) or pieces of food to push food onto your fork. Do not lick your knife or eat off it; the fork and spoon are the only utensils that should go in your mouth. Use your knife to aid your fork in picking up your food.

19. If you are the host, everyone starts to eat when you do, unless you release them to begin eating. "Go ahead, don't wait on me." If you are not the host, do not start to eat until your host does. I have frequently seen salespeople start the minute the food is placed in front of them, only to look up and see everyone staring at them. Digging into your food before the host lowers your credibility.

20. When eating soup, follow your host's example. If he eats it all, you may eat it all, or you may leave some. Old tradition recommends that you leave a little soup in your bowl, so you do not appear greedy or starved for food. Do not lower your head to the plate. Spoon soup away from you; lift the spoon to your mouth. Do not slurp; sip from the corner of the spoon, not the

tip of the spoon. Do not blow on hot soup or dunk bread in soup. If eating soup from a cup, use a spoon to eat vegetables or noodles before lifting the cup to drink the remainder of the broth. When finished place the spoon on the saucer under the soup bowl or in the middle of the bowl with the spoon handle to the right.

21. Do not finish the last bite of anything in a shared dish (oyster, shrimp, brochette, etc.) unless the host insists. Then it is rude to refuse unless you are full, sick, or you just don't care if you are rude.

22. If cheese is served, do not pass the cheese tray around more than once. Do not take more than three kinds of cheese from a tray and do not take seconds. You will appear greedy and gauche to people who know proper manners. If you must cut the cheese, cut it so that it does not change the shape of the cheese and cut only enough for yourself. *Please*, do not make a cheese and cracker sandwich. Again, tradition says a second helping of cheese means you did not get enough to eat.

23. Lastly, what to do if your dinner guest is choking on food. This happened to me and it could happen to you. A person who is choking needs immediate attention. Call 911 and someone needs to immediately apply the Heimlich maneuver to the choking person. Everyone needs to learn the Heimlich maneuver.

Study the place setting illustration on page 50 so that you will have operational knowledge of the different pieces of flatware and glassware found in a place setting.

CHAPTER 7

TIPS FOR GOOD BUSINESS CONVERSATION

Listening is as important as talking. If you're a good listener, people often compliment you for being a good conversationalist.

—Jesse Ventura

onversations can be regarded as social conversation (an exchange of pleasantries and basic personal information), and business conversation (discussing the client's needs and sales agenda). A typical lunch or dinner meeting would begin with social conversation—small talk—followed with your sales conversation.

Here are 10 conversational tips:

1. **Expand your range of conversation topics.** Be willing to go where you are uncomfortable and try new things; teach the butterflies in your stomach to fly in formation. New experiences will increase your pool of knowledge, making you an interesting person capable of stimulating conversation. Life is growth—or it is nothing.

2. **Ask questions.** When your guest asks you a question or your opinion, show your interest in them by asking the same question or opinion. Note: It is wise to learn the opinions of others before you give your own.

3. **Nod your head.** Studies reveal people will talk 66% more if you reinforce what they are saying by nodding your head.

4. **Memorize a list of topics.** Find common areas of interest to talk about: travel, family, business, sports, hobbies, charities, and current events. Learn to ask questions about these topics.

5. **Do not talk about yourself.** Talking incessantly about yourself tells your prospect or client you have an inflated ego. When a client asks a question about you, give him a brief, courteous answer, and then subtly turn the conversation back onto your client.

6. **Ask personal questions carefully.** Never ask what you would not want to answer yourself. Questions about a person's relationships, religion, and money can make a prospect or client uncomfortable.

7. **Do not share intimate information.** A business meeting is not the place to reveal the private details of your life. Treat your client as a business relationship, not as your buddy or confidante.

8. **Focus on positive topics.** Do not discuss politics unless the prospect introduces it; then mostly listen and do not agree. Avoid discussion of tragedies. Do not talk about a recent divorce, the death of a pet, or how magnificently you wrecked your Mercedes.

9. **Do not have side conversations.** Side conversations are inappropriate and rude. No one wants to stare at the backside of someone's head while the person sitting beside them engages in private dialogue at the table. If you are sitting in the middle of two people,

lean slightly backwards to include others in your conversation. Draw others into the conversation by making eye contact with two or more guests as you talk.

10. **Do not reveal the internal workings of your company.** Divulging the behind-the-scenes affairs of your company or private information about your boss and coworkers tells a client you are not trustworthy.

CHAPTER 8

THE RIGHT WAY TO INTRODUCE THE BUSINESS AGENDA

Timing is everything in life and golf.

—*Arnold Palmer*

"I just want to eat! I don't want to see a storyboard of your proposal."

A successful lunch or business meeting typically begins with guest introductions and social conversation, followed with an enjoyable meal, and afterwards the business agenda is presented. However, lunch and dinner business meetings are not all the same; external factors can alter the order and flow of your meeting.

There are no hard and fast rules on how and when to introduce your business agenda, but there are general rules that you should follow.

To begin with, do not pull sales material out when there is food on the table; this is the biggest mistake I see when salespeople present their materials. It is difficult at lunch or dinner to fight presentation materials while plates of food are in front of you.

Do not present anything before you have ordered because there will always be a break in concentration. There is too much happening between the time you first sit down and when you order your food to achieve a stream of consciousness. Use this down-time to establish rapport with your prospect or client.

Consider the length of your presentation. If it is short, perhaps you can present your materials after you place your order and before the food arrives. If you choose to present your materials between ordering and the service of the food, make sure you complete your presentation before the food arrives, or at least finish with the physical materials, because once the food comes, the papers, laptops or other visuals come off the table. If you are not sure you can complete the presentation—*then wait.*

As a rule, the best time to do rapport building and fact-finding is during the meal, and the best time to present your visuals is after the meal is completed. I like to introduce my presentation and materials after the plates have been cleared, over coffee. You may have to ask the waiter to clear the plates so you can get started—*do not hesitate to do this.* If it is a lunch meeting, it may be best to go to your prospect's or client's office after lunch to present your materials. As I said, there are no hard and fast rules—just principles you should not violate.

Here are some examples of lunch and dinner presentation mistakes.

Jon was presenting a proposal based on a consulting project he did for a client. He invited the client to an early dinner at a restaurant where Jon was well known. Jon let his client know that they were going to cover his proposal at dinner. Almost the moment they were seated, Jon handed the physical proposal to his client. His client was excited about the proposal and he dove into the material. Then came the interruptions: Every time the waiter came to the table (to pour water, to take their orders, to pour their wine, and to refresh their wine glasses), Jon and his client had to put aside their materials and conversation to address the waiter. When food was served, Jon had to completely end his presentation.

Fortunately (luckily), Jon's dinner meeting had a happy ending. He got the sale, but it was not based on the prospect's understanding of the material presented during dinner.

Dale took a qualified prospect to lunch to talk about buying equipment for his bank. Dale's prospect was fully aware of the lunch agenda. However, Dale and his prospect were such good friends they basically caught up on each other's life during lunch. Dale waited until lunch was over to talk about business, but as he was about to introduce his materials, his prospect looked at his watch and said, "I've got to get back to the bank." The prospect never bought Dale's equipment.

Always find out how much time your prospect or client can spend with you. If the prospect is short on time, you need to know this at the beginning of meeting, not when the meal is finished, and you ordered coffee. When you sit down at the dining table ask your prospect or client, "Are you in a hurry?" If he says "yes," adjust your presentation. If he says "no," go with Plan A. Better to break some of the other rules than to not get your story told.

Choose where you will sit at the table based upon the material you will be presenting. A four-top or two-top table allows you to sit across from the prospect so you can oversee the materials. A large four-top means you need to sit closer to the prospect, corner to corner, and not across. Otherwise, you cannot control how the prospect looks at the material.

I hate using laptops or PowerPoint in a public restaurant. It feels weird and awkward to put your computer on the dining table and go through a slide show with people dining all around you. Besides, there are issues with light, electricity, speed, and convenience. A good old-fashioned paper presentation is usually best in a one-on-one or one-on-two presentation. It is okay to make mistakes during your presentation—but correct them the next time and use common sense.

Here is a wrap-up of rules for presenting material at a lunch or dinner meeting:

1. Do not present material while food is on the table.

2. Do not start and stop your presentation while food is being served.

3. Do not use your laptop in a public restaurant.

4. Do not hand material out until you are ready to go over it.

5. Sit where you can control the materials.

6. If you are the one presenting materials, follow the rules (Chapter 3) about restaurant selection.

CHAPTER 9

INTRODUCTION TO WINE TERMS

An appreciation of fine wine is a part of a
sophisticated, adventurous approach to life.

—*Marvin Shanken*

"Is this the wine you selected at random?"

During my 30-year business career I have heard numerous discussions about wine. You should familiarize yourself with wine terms so that you can, in addition to ordering wine at a restaurant like a pro, engage in discussions about wine intelligently. If a prospect or client uses wine terms incorrectly—do not correct them. Instead, buy them my book *Doing Business at the Table* as a gift.

THE CORRECT USE OF WINE TERMS

1. **Attack**—The first impression the wine makes as it enters your mouth. Usually the fruit is represented in the attack since our sweet taste buds are on the front of our tongues.

2. **Balanced**—This is wine which has no characteristic stronger than the others. It is a balance of fruit, acid, and tannin. Balance is the number one standard for great wine.

3. **Complex**—A wine with a number of flavors and qualities (all good). It is the opposite of "one dimensional."

4. **Finish**—The last impression the wine makes as it leaves your mouth when it is swallowed. Usually, the longer the finish, the better the wine. The opposite of a long finish would be an "aftertaste" which is the flavor that remains in the back of the throat and nasal passages after the wine has been drunk. Usually this is the sign of a wine in poor condition.

5. **Nose**—The aroma of the wine; the way it smells.

6. **Palate**—The way the wine feels in your mouth or the weight of the wine in your mouth.

7. **Weight**—The texture and heft of a wine. Wines can be thick or thin, heavy, or light.

8. **Light-bodied**—Many inexpensive white wines (under $15/bottles) are light-bodied. For red wines, this means not much tannin or acid. Beaujolais Nouveau wine is light bodied. Full-bodied red wine is the opposite. Most high-priced California cabernet sauvignons are full-bodied. Light-bodied white wine means a lack of acidity. Most Grand Cru white burgundies have good acidity and are full-bodied.

9. **Good Acidity**—On the nose, good acidity is usually reflected by strong fruit scents, especially citrus, crisp apple, and ripe pineapple. Good acidity on the palate is mouthwatering—like biting a lemon. Acidity is reflected on the sides of your tongue. Lack of acidity gives wine a flabby characteristic and a watery finish. If the wine seems to lack vitality, it is usually a lack of acidity.

10. **Baked**—When there is an extremely hot growing season with little rainfall, the grapes may get burned. This makes the wine smell and taste earthy and "hot." This is most often seen where wine is produced in hot climates.

11. **Bitter**—Obviously, a taste detected in the mouth. Its causes are legion; however, it makes a wine undrinkable.

12. **Coarse**—A descriptor used to describe a rough or "coarse" wine. It shows a lack of sophistication and breeding, usually a characteristic of poor or indifferent winemaking. Many great young wines may seem coarse; but they are not, they are immature wines that need development, much like a child versus a hopelessly coarse 60-year-old adult.

13. **Corked**—An often-overused descriptor. It is caused by the mold, TCA. It has a very distinct wet cardboard smell and will only get worse as the bacterium multiplies during contact with air. If there is any doubt whether a wine is corked, let it sit. If the smell gets worse, it is corked.

14. **Maderized**—A heavy, flat smell marked by the presence of metal elements and the lack of fresh fruit. It is caused by age or exposure to oxygen and is usually associated with "oxidized" which is an over exposure to oxygen. In red wine, it is a burned metal smell. In white wine, usually the color turns deeper yellow and the nose is metallic.

15. **Spritz or Spritzy**—This is a flaw in non-sparkling wine. It is created by refermentation starting once the wine is bottled. CO_2 is released in fermentation and the wine, once bottled, cannot let the gas escape. You can recognize it by a slight prickle on the tongue.

WINE WORLD RECORDS

1. Most expensive bottle of wine: 1787 Château Lafite, sold at Christie's, London, in December 1985, for £105,000.

2. Largest flute of sparkling wine 6' 7", filled with 16.5 litres (4.4 gallons) of Asti in Umbria, Italy, in May 2008.

3. Most people treading grapes at once: 540 employees of British American Tobacco at the Pepper Tree Winery in Hunter Valley, Australia, in April 2005.

4. Largest Wine tasting: 5,095 tasters at the Plazas de Toros bullring in Aranda de Duero, Spain in September 2006.

5. Most wine glasses held in one hand: 39 by Flipino Reymond Adina in October 2007 at Quatre-Gats restaurant, Barcelona.

–Guinness World Records 2011

WINEMAKING TERMS

In conjunction with the wine terms that relate to drinking wine, there are also specific terms about winemaking. Knowledge of both set of terms will help you participate intelligently in a discussion about wines. Again, if your prospect or client misuses these terms—do not correct him.

1. **Terroir**—In the old world, terroir refers to the combination of soil, microclimate, altitude, and sun exposure. It is regarded as the most important factor in determining a great wine.

2. **Green Harvesting**—In the summer, long before harvest, bunches of grapes are cut from the vines. This forces the plant to concentrate its energy on ripening the remaining fruit and increasing its flavor.

3. **Effeuillage**—Trimming the vines to expose the grapes to sunlight for optimum ripeness and to the wind so the grapes remain dry and avoid rot.

4. **Field Taste**—The Maître de Chai (winemaker) goes into the vineyard to taste the grapes and chew the seeds. This determines their sugar content so that harvest can be scheduled.

5. **Harvest**—Old World tradition is that the grapes are harvested by hand. This must be done in the shortest possible time when the grapes are at their peak, usually early in the morning.

6. **Crushing or Pressing**—Grapes for red wine are fed into the crusher, keeping the skins and seeds. The result is called a "must." For some white wine, the skins and seeds are removed, and the grapes are gently pressed into a "juice."

7. **Fermentation**—The juice is put into steel tanks, oak barrels, or a "barrique" which hold 25 to 30 cases of wine. Yeast is added to ferment the juice. Alcohol is created as the sugars break down. The juice begins turning into wine.

8. **Punching the Cap**—The cap is the lid of skins that float to the top of the "must" for red wine. The "cap" must be kept in contact with the liquid. A process of "punching the cap" or pushing it down into the wine must be performed repeatedly.

9. **Fining**—In this step, an agent such as egg whites is added to the wine. This causes the sediment or "lees" to settle on the bottom of the barrel.

10. **Racking**—A process of filtering the wine to remove bacteria or microorganisms. In this stage the wine is pumped from one barrel to another barrel. The remaining "lees" are removed. When correctly done the wine gains character. Performed incorrectly, the result is weak wine. This is a controversial step that not every winemaker practices.

11. **Secondary Fermentation**—Malic acid in the wine is converted into lactic acid. While this process is done with all red wines, only some white wines go through this step. In white wine, it reduces the crispness of the wine and adds a buttery flavor.

12. **Barrel Aging**—The wine is put into oak or redwood barrels. The wine soaks up the character of the wood which adds flavor and bouquet. The process can last from months to many years.

13. **Assemblage**—If a blend is being created, this is where the winemaker assembles different wines to fulfill the original concept of the wine.

14. **Barrel Tasting**—During aging, the winemaker tastes the wine to check its progress. When the wine is clear, and the winemaker believes all the components are at their peak (taste, color, bouquet, and feel) the fermentation is complete.

15. **Methode Champenoise**—Champagne goes through an additional fermentation that creates carbon dioxide. The bottles are stored upside down and every day they are turned and then slammed "riddled" back into their holding rack forcing the sediment into the neck of the bottle. The bottles are then turned upside down and there are necks frozen. In the final step, the carbon dioxide inside forces out the ice along with the sediment. The bottles are quickly re-corked with the remaining carbon dioxide inside.

16. **Bottling**—The wine is bottled. In some cases, the wine is allowed to "bottle age." If this is the case, the cellarmaster determines when the wine is ready. Otherwise, the wine is transported for sale.

17. **Libation** (ly-BAY-shun), noun—1. The act of pouring a liquid (usually wine) either on the ground or on a victim in a sacrifice to some deity; also, the wine or liquid that is thus poured out. 2. A beverage, especially an alcoholic beverage.

18. **Dumb Wine**—Describes, in general, a closed wine (particularly red) that lacks a distinctive nose or aroma. More precisely, it refers also to a certain period or phase ("dumb phase") of an age-worthy wine that is past its youth, but not yet at its full maturity, and simply does not taste right or smell correct at the time. This phenomenon happens for unknown, unpredictable reasons; it is as if the wine

has hit its adolescent—awkward stage—yet still has plenty of potential for growth. A "numb" wine on the other hand, has a muted or non-existent scent and flavors and has no potential for maturity. It is wine equivalent of the lazy son who never grows up and wallows in his parents' basement. Ironically, wines often become numb from improper storage in basement wine cellars.

19. **Fiasco**—In wine parlance, a fiasco is a typical Italian-style bottle, usually with a rounded body and base, covered with a close-fitting straw basket. *Boring.* But the real mystery is how this word for a wine bottle became a commonly known term that describes an utter mess. The bottle is first mentioned in a 1350 collection of novellas called Decameron. In 1855, fiasco was used in Italian theater slang to describe a failure on stage, and ten years later, in general, for any dismal flop. It has been suggested that Venetian glass-crafters tossed aside imperfect pieces to be made later into common flasks (or fiascos), this possibly explains today's usage of fiasco. But according to an Italian dictionary, fare il fiasco is used to mean "to play a game so that the one that loses will pay the fiasco," in other words, buy the next bottle of wine. *This plausibly connects the word with the notion of costly mistake. —Casey Dooley*

George Bernard Shaw, who was noted for many things, gave us a great thought, "A mind the caliber of mine cannot derive its nutriment from cows. I must have wine."

AGED WINE WORLD RECORDS

1. World's oldest bottle of wine: dating from about 325 A.D., the glass amphora was found in1867 inside a Roman stone sarcophagus excavated near Speyer, Germany. The bottle is displayed at the Historiches Museum der Pfalz in Speyer.

2. World's oldest grapevine: It is said to be a 400-year-old vine in the town of Maribor in Slovenia. A varietal called Îametovka, it still bears grapes harvested for wine.

3. Oldest winery in France: Archeologists are excavating a site dating from the first century B.C. in the town of Aspirian, located in the Languedoc region. Remarkably advanced, it features ceramic fermentation tanks buried in the earth, around which water flowed to maintain constant temperature, similar to modern stainless-steel tank systems.

–Wine Enthusiast, April 2011

CHAPTER 10

ORDERING WINE LIKE AN EXPERT

---

*Drinking wine was not snobbism or a sign
of sophistication nor a cult; it was as natural
as eating and to me as necessary.*

—Ernest Hemingway

A s a CEO, business owner, and entrepreneur, I felt lunch and dinner meetings could help me build rapport with my prospects and clients; and consequently, increase my bottom-line. I was trying to be the kind of person with whom my prospects wanted to do business. Wine became an important element in entertaining my prospects and clients and my interest in wine was sparked. As the host of frequent lunch and dinner business meetings, I wanted to know how to order, taste, and accept wine in a restaurant. I made a lot of mistakes along the way, and I still do, but through the years I have gained a wealth of knowledge about wine. In fact, I am known internationally as a wine personality. At one time, my personal wine cellar stored over 60,000 bottles, and yet, I still learn something new about wine almost daily.

Learn the information in my book and you can be the expert at the table and impress your prospects and clients with your above-average knowledge of wine.

Let's start by discussing the restaurant wine list.

Whether you are at a big restaurant or a small eatery, they all have one thing in common: a selection of white and red wine with varying prices. This is where you start; if you know nothing about wine, pick a price range. If the waiter is skilled or there is a sommelier, their job is to get you to spend more than your budget. Don't let them down! For four people, a $100 bottle of wine only adds $25 per person.

Once you have established a price range, pick a color—red or white. The first rule on wine color selection is to pick what you like. The second rule is: red meat equals red wine; fish and seafood equal white wine.

Let us say you have decided on a red wine and your price range is $50-$100. If you do not recognize any of the wines on the list (this happens to me frequently, so it must happen to you), ask the sommelier or waiter to explain the wines. Say something like, "My companion is having the duck and I am having the lamb." I then point to my price range on the menu and I say, "What would you recommend in this range?" I point at the price while holding the menu between me and my guest. I have discreetly involved my guest in the decision process, and I have subtly asked the sommelier or waiter to help me select an appropriate wine to complement our meal.

As you get better at understanding wine, you will learn to ask questions like, "Is this wine fruit forward or more subtle?" If you know which wine you want, then forget everything I have told you—*and go for it*.

DOWN AND DIRTY TIPS THAT ENHANCE YOUR FOOD WITH THE WINE.

There is a principal called "synergy of wine and food." It is like ketchup and french fries; they are better together than by themselves. The proper wine will enhance the food, making steak, chicken, and fish taste better. Here is a simple guide to help you pair wine and food:

- **Light dishes deserve light wine**—Mild, light dishes like halibut and vegetable-based pastas work well with Pinot Blanc, Chablis, and Ribola Gaia (Italian grape).

- **Medium-bodied dishes deserve medium-bodied wines**—Grilled seafood, swordfish, salmon, octopus, scallops, chicken, etc. work well with Sauvignon Blanc, Roussanne, Sancerre, Italian blends, and Viognier. My personal favorite is Bordeaux Blanc.

- **Full-bodied foods deserve full-bodied wines**—Creamy pastas, spicy seafood dishes, strong-flavored fish (like sardines), barbecued chicken, etc. work well with Burgundies, American Chardonnay, Hermitage Blanc, and most Rhône whites.

Want to drink red wine?

- **Medium-bodied red wine works with medium dishes**—Pork: grilled, chops or roasts; BBQ chicken, salmon, gamebirds, quail, pheasant, and squab work well with red Burgundies and Pinot Noirs from almost anywhere, as do lighter Sangiovese and older Bordeaux.

- **Full-bodied dishes work with full-bodied wines**—Beef: roasted, grilled or the ribs; lamb: roasted, chops, or grilled, and pork ribs work with Zinfandel, Bordeaux blends, Cabernets, Merlots, Shiraz, Rhône reds, Malbec. Think big reds with fatty meat.

If your guests order a wide variety of food, Pinot Noir is your safest bet. It goes with almost everything. You get the idea—*if you don't, order beer!*

Now comes the wine!

The waiter pulls the cork. If he breaks the cork and there is cork in your wine, don't be a wimp—*refuse the wine!* The waiter or sommelier screwed up and you should not have to pick cork out of your teeth. Tell the waiter, "I'd rather have a fresh bottle that has no cork in it." Many times, I have seen customers accept poor wine service. It is not your fault that pieces of cork are floating in your wine—*do not accept the bottle.*

Let us assume that the cork comes out in one piece—*yay!* Now the waiter or sommelier should smell the cork. If the cork smells bad, they should take the wine back and get a new bottle. If they do not take the wine back, you should ask them to replace the bottle.

A bad smelling cork equals a bad wine 95 percent of the time.

I could describe all the smells you should look for when evaluating wine, but simply put, if it smells bad, say, "The cork smells bad." You should still taste the wine—but if the cork smells bad, expect the worst.

Research says of all wines using a real, natural cork, five percent of them will have a bad cork that taints the wine. That means one in twenty bottles is bad. This is commonly referred to as a "corked" wine. There is mold (forget the name, you'll never remember it) that causes the wine to smell like wet cardboard. Some people are more sensitive than others to a wine that smells bad. If you smell anything other than fruit, minerals, nuts, or flowers, send the wine back (occasionally there will be no odor or a light vinegar smell—these are both okay). Most people cannot recognize specifically what is wrong with the wine; they just know that it smells bad. That is enough reason for you to send the bottle back!

Now comes the resistance from your waiter or sommelier. Your wine smells bad, you ask for a new bottle, and they say, "It smells alright to me!" You are the customer; the waiter's or sommelier's job is to make sure you have a pleasant dining experience. Politely consider their comment about the "corked wine" and then ask for a new bottle. The restaurant can return the wine to the distributor and the distributor can send it back to the winery.

One night I had dinner with Warren Winiarski, the owner of Stags' Leap Winery. We ordered a bottle of his Stags' Leap chardonnay. The wine was "corked," and we got another bottle (maybe two). Corked wine is not the customer's fault—and it happens to everyone.

Let's talk about tasting the wine. The waiter or sommelier pours a small taste of wine in your glass. Before you drink it, smell the cork and smell the wine. When you taste the wine, do not gargle with it; but do draw air over the wine in your mouth and swallow a little. An experienced taster knows by "color" and "nose" if the wine is good. If it does not taste good—*send it back*!

Now you have smelled the cork, you nosed the wine, and you have tasted it. You say to the server, "that's fine." The ritual is over, and it is time to enjoy the wine with the food. If you are having fun and you order a second bottle, you should repeat the ritual with a clean glass. If you are a real purist, everyone should get new glasses with a new bottle of wine—even if it is the same wine. I don't always do this as it seems a waste with a $25 bottle of wine.

Do you tip on the wine?

Follow your company's policy. Most people say adjust the tip based on the price of the wine and quality of service. I sometimes follow this practice, or I may just tip on the food and give a separate cash tip to the sommelier. I tip more in New York than in Clarksville, Tennessee. No one on their deathbed ever said, "I tipped too much."

Do not let wine intimidate you. In the beginning, no one orders wine at a restaurant naturally or without making some mistakes. It takes time and effort to become an aficionado of wine. Expose yourself to a variety of wines; if your standard go-to is white wine, try a light-bodied Pinot Noir and then a full-bodied Burgundy. Subscribe to wine magazines; learn about wine and food pairings. Wine tastings are a great way to familiarize yourself with different wines and exchange conversation with other wine enthusiasts. Keep a notebook of the wines that you like. With your new awareness and with practice you will get comfortable ordering wine for you and your guests. Your prospect or client will notice your dining savvy and you will gain their confidence and respect.

CHAPTER 11

THE CUSTOM OF TOASTING ETIQUETTE

*It usually takes three weeks
to prepare a good impromptu speech.*

—*Mark Twain*

"Do you want the bad cheap wine or the really fantastic expensive wine?"

The Greeks were the first to toast. It was a remedy for poisoning. They all drank at the same time from the same pot, pitcher, or carafe. In addition, they would spill a little of each other's wine into someone else's goblet to further ensure that no one was up to no good.

I have been to dinners where I should have done that.

Next were the Romans with their toast tradition. The word "toast" comes from the Roman custom of dropping a piece of burnt toast into the wine to filter out impurities and help settle the solids in the wine. The making of wine today is more sophisticated; the burnt toast is gone, but the name remains the same.

Shakespeare continued the tradition when he wrote in Hamlet about the custom of toasting and draining the cup. "It is a custom more honored in the breach than the observance." In other words, it was the custom to drink all the wine in the glass in one motion, but few people did it. *Who knew Shakespeare was Irish!*

There are many customs and traditions associated with toasts. Amy Vanderbilt's *Complete Book of Etiquette* offers a section on the protocol of toasts. Her best advice was, in my opinion, to "keep it brief."

My top advice is Don't ridicule someone with a toast in front of your boss. My other advice is: *The less you drink in a business setting, the better.*

I try to remember ten good toasts. That way, I am prepared to recognize someone or provide some entertainment. Here are my ten favorite toasts depending on the occasion, the moment, and how much wine I have enjoyed.

1. "I might wish you wealth and I might wish you health, or that good fortune would caress you, but wealth might bring sorrow, and health might fade tomorrow, so I'll simply say, 'God bless you.'"

2. "In water one sees one's own face, but in wine [red wine] one beholds the heart of another." —French proverb

3. "Give me wine to wash me clean from the weather-stains of care."—Ralph Waldo Emerson

4. "My heart is as full as my glass when I drink to you, my friends."

5. "The taste of good wine is remembered long after the price is forgotten."

6. "May the road rise up to meet you. May the wind always be at your back. May the sunshine warm upon your face; the rains fall softly upon your fields, and may you be in Heaven an hour before the devil knows you're gone."—Irish blessing

7. "For a happy life, don't lie, don't cheat, and don't drink, but you may lie with the one you love, try to cheat death, and drink with family and friends."

8. "This above all: to thine own self be true, And it must follow, as the night the day, Thou canst not then be false to any man."—Shakespeare

9. "To old friends and new friends, may we meet again, and the best of the past be the worst of our future."—Tom Black

10. "It was a woman that drove me to drink and I never even wrote to thank her."—W.C. Fields

There are toasting customs that everyone should observe. First, the person making the toast should stand and hold their glass chest high and look people in the eye when you toast; it is polite. It is permissible for the toaster to tap their glass to get everyone's attention. After the toast you may clink glasses with the two people seated next to you, or clink glasses with everyone within reach; however, old superstition says if you miss a glass, you will spend a year without sex. Touching the glass adds another element to the experience, sound tickling another one of our senses.

A toast should be upbeat, to the point, and always respectful of other diners. Here are some *don'ts* for toasting in a business environment.

1. Do not toast yourself. If you are the recipient of the toast, do not stand, do not raise your glass, and do not drink from your glass. Simply respond, "Thank you. That's very thoughtful."

2. Do not toast with water. It is considered bad luck and bad form.

3. Do not toast at breakfast meetings. If anyone asks you to toast at a breakfast meeting, you may politely decline.

4. Do not use notecards to give a toast in a formal environment.

5. Do not use stand-up comedy to give a toast in a business environment. It is not appropriate; in fact, I have often seen humor backfire when toasting.

6. Do not ever use a ribald toast; do not use profanity or sexual inferences. No one enjoys being embarrassed by off-color humor.

7. Do not ever give a back-handed toast. For example: "Congratulations, John. You got lucky on this one." Taking a jab at someone at a professional gathering is in poor taste.

8. Do not crash your glass into someone else's glass. A simple touch of the rim is all that is required.

9. Do not offer a toast in response to someone else's toast. Do not toast someone who was not toasted in the original toast. Subsequent toasts diminish the original toast and it is ineffective to have a series of toasts at a business dinner.

10. Do not say anything you do not want outsiders to hear because meetings in a restaurant are never entirely private.

Now you can toast with the best of them. And I raise a toast to you for your love and interest in doing a great job at the business table.

Here is a closing thought from my friend and mentor, the late Michael Broadbent:

"The aristocrat of the table, the gentleman of the cellar ... the deeply knowledgeable is rarely, if ever, a snob. He stands ready to answer any question but bores no one with useless information."

APPROPRIATE AFTER-DINNER DRINKS

The toasts have been presented; wine and the dinner were served. The evening so far has been superb. Now it is time to enjoy a rousing after-dinner drink. Here are some of my favorites:

Port—A Portuguese fortified wine. It is a sweet red wine; traditionally it was served as an after-dinner drink and not with dessert. It has a nutty, raisin flavor with a sweet finish. It often has coffee, caramel, and smoky notes. Port is best served with a dark chocolate dessert.

Sweet Wines—A variety of sweet wines served with dessert or cheese. The most common ones are Sauternes, late harvest wines, Tokaji, Ice wines, Trockenbeerenauslese, Muscat de Beaumes, Vin Santo, etc. These wines come from every country that produces wine. Try a few and find the ones you like.

Sweet Sherry—Made in Spain from raisins and then fortified. It is stronger than most dessert wines.

Brandy, Armagnac, or Cognac—In general, they have a whiskey flavor with a hint of fruit. It is made with distilled fruit (apples, grapes, blackberries, etc.).

Single Malt Scotch—A whiskey made from malted barley; made exclusively in Scotland. It is usually drunk without additives (I like that!) and it is considered a digestif (helps with digestion). Flavors include smoky, peaty, and honey notes.

Liqueurs—Basically, sweetened liquors often contain lower alcohol levels. There are too many liqueurs to list; popular ones are Amari, Chartreuse, Galliano, Grappa, and Ouzo. They all have different flavors: coffee liqueurs, berry liqueurs, chocolate liqueurs, cream liqueurs, flower, fruit, herbal, nut flavored and honey flavored liqueurs. Try them until you find the ones you like.

CHAPTER 12

TOP RESTAURANT GUIDES AND RATINGS

We all eat, and it would be a sad waste
of opportunity to eat badly.

—*Anna Thomas*

W hile nothing takes the place of dining in a restaurant before you book a lunch or dinner meeting, there are guides and rating systems that can help you evaluate thousands of restaurants locally and nationally.

The most comprehensive rating system is Zagat (pronounced "zuh-gat"). Zagat offers restaurant guides and reviews in both a hard copy and online for all major U.S. cities and will rate the restaurant on service, quality of service, food, price, and décor. In addition, the location, hours, and a basic description of the restaurants are included. Zagat ranks restaurants that appeal to baby boomers, as well as the X or Y generation. Zagat ratings are compiled by people who patron the restaurants; it is not one critic's opinion, but the opinion of lots of people who consistently dine in restaurants. More importantly, their ratings are published annually, which gives me more confidence over a review that was done two or three years ago.

Where the Locals Eat publishes a directory of the best restaurants in America with reviews in 10,000 restaurants in

50 states and more than 1,000 cities. Their reviews are based on phone surveys of prominent businesspeople in the community which seems to be quite accurate. Their restaurant directory is available online, in hard copy, and on their LocalEats app. You can find them at www.wherethelocalseat.com.

For nearly a half-century, Mobil Travel Guide has provided travelers with the most objective, most disciplined ratings for restaurants in North America. It is a proven, time-tested gold standard for rating a restaurant's quality of food, service, and atmosphere.

What about all these stars and diamonds?

Mobil Travel Guide is the originator of the prestigious Five-Star ratings program. A five-star restaurant reflects the best-of-the-best in hospitality excellence and are typically very expensive; the second-tier rating of four-stars is also a good dining experience. Very few restaurants achieve the four- or five-star designation; 12-15 restaurants in the U.S. may get a five-star rating annually. The Mobil Star ratings and certifications provide travelers with trustworthy recommendations supported by actual physical inspections. Their field staff inspects thousands of restaurants each year. During each restaurant inspection, hundreds of criteria are considered. Hospitality and travel industry professionals respect the Mobil Star rating and certification system. Consumers have put their faith in it for over 40 years as they determine where to dine.

The Automobile Association uses a system of diamonds. Five Diamonds is the highest award, and there are very few Five-Diamond restaurants. I find it interesting when the same restaurant is rated, Mobil Star rating is higher or lower than the Automobile Association Diamond rating. Not every critic agrees; take that into consideration.

In case you are planning to entertain clients abroad, the Michelin Guide publishes restaurant ratings for England and Europe, as well as, New York, Las Vegas, Chicago, Los Angeles, and now San Francisco. Michelin Guide's top rating for a restaurant is three stars. While there are very few European Three-Star restaurants, they outnumber Five-Diamond or Five-Star restaurants in the United States.

Michelin has been in the business of evaluating and recommending restaurants and hotels for over a century. The Michelin System is obviously biased toward French-style fine dining. They employ full-time professional inspectors who anonymously visit restaurants and hotels and evaluate them on a range of criteria. Their evaluation process has been honed over time to identify consistently high-quality establishments to suit a range of budgets and diversity of styles and cuisines.

The Michelin Guide uses a system of symbols to identify the best restaurants within each price category. Michelin stars are based on five criteria:

- The quality of the products
- The mastery of flavor and cooking
- The "personality" of the cuisine
- The value for the "money
- The consistency between visits

Michelin stars are awarded to restaurants offering the finest cooking. Stars represent only what is on the plate. They do not take into consideration interior decoration, service quality, or table settings. Their grading system is:

 * = A very good restaurant in its category

 ** = Excellent cooking and worth a detour

 *** = Exceptional cuisine and worth the journey

The Michelin Guide is available both online and in hard copy.

When James Beard, the famous American Chef, was asked what his favorite restaurant was, he answered, "One where I am known."

This is so true!

Frankly, more important to me than the restaurant rating is how I am treated as a customer. If the service is good, the waiter is attentive, and I get a table located in a quiet corner of the restaurant, that is the start of a productive business meeting.

CHAPTER 13

THE MENU: CUTS OF MEAT, FOWL, FISH, CHEESES, AND MORE

To eat is a necessity.
But to eat intelligently is an art.

—*Francois del la RocheFoucauld*

"It is way too much food. That's why we charge way too much money.

I **learned** to drink beer in college, and I did not like dry wine. I graduated from college; I was a typical restaurant patron, ordering prime rib at Steak and Ale and a burger and fries at Applebee's. I knew little about the different cuts of meat and fish, or even the vegetables offered on upscale restaurant menus. As a young salesperson, my boss told me that I would be taking bankers to lunch and dinner. I realized as the host, in addition to knowing how to order wine for my prospects and clients, I needed to know how to navigate an upscale restaurant menu.

It became my lifetime quest to be a "gentleman of the table."

The following information will help you appreciate the many cuts, grades, and quality of the meats, fowl, fish, cheese, and other food items that commonly appear on menus. This is not a complete list, but rather the offering you will see commonly on restaurant menus.

I think you will enjoy finally understanding what you are eating.

BEEF CLASSIFICATIONS AND GRADING TERMS

Certified Humane—Certification given by the Humane Farm Animal Care (a non-profit organization) which involves handling, feed, living conditions, and health care of farm animals.

Certified Organic—All feed that is given to cattle is grown organically; no growth hormones or antibiotics are used. They are certified by the USDA's Agricultural Marketing Service.

Certified Angus Beef—About 90% of the beef we eat is Angus, however, "Certified Angus" means that it has USDA requirements for marbling, maturity, and weight.

Grain Finished—Cattle finish the last four to six months of their life in feed lots eating grain. This is mostly corn ("corn-fed") but can be other grains like wheat, barley, and soybeans. Grain-fed beef usually have more fat and are thus juicier.

Grass Finished—Many times, cattle spent their whole life grazing on pasture grass. This means leaner beef and less juicy cuts of beef.

Waqyu Beef—Also known as Kobe beef. This beef has a high fat content and is extremely tender. This beef has their origins in Japan, hence the name Kobe. This is an expensive cut of beef.

Aged Beef—Beef can be aged in two ways, wet-aged and dry-aged. Wet-aged is sent from the slaughterhouse in vacuum sealed bags and is aged in its own juices. Dry-aged beef is just that, it is aged without a cover in a refrigerator at 35° and 60% humidity. While the beef ages, it loses up to 20% of its moisture. Aging intensifies flavor and tenderness and makes the beef more expensive.

BEEF CUTS

During the butchering of the cow, the animal is first divided into primal cuts. These are large pieces of meat separated from the carcass. Do not confuse primal and prime cuts—they are quite different.

Different countries and regions have different names and shapes for different cuts of beef. You do not need to know everything, but you should know the general area of the cow the meat comes from and what its flavor and texture will be when you order it.

There are 8 primal cuts of beef:

1. Chuck
2. Rib
3. Loin
4. Flank
5. Short Plate
6. Brisket
7. Shank

After that, they become sub-primal cuts. The most expensive cuts are in the middle of the cow. The further from the head and feet; the more tender the meat.

My mom used to say, "There are more steaks than you can shake a stick at."

Prime Rib—The highest grade of beef by the USDA. It has the highest degree of marbling referred to as "abundant." Prime beef represents 3% or less of all beef.

Choice Beef—The grade below prime, also based primarily on marbling. About 30% of beef is graded "choice."

Tenderloin Steak—The tenderest steak of all. The whole tenderloin can be cooked as a roast and cut individually, or you may order it as an individual steak, usually grilled or roasted in the oven. It has less fat and flavor and it is more tender than other cuts of steak.

Filet Mignon—A French term for steak cut from the center of the tenderloin. These steaks are generally 2-inches thick and are known for their tenderness, not their flavor. They usually have less fat than other popular steaks.

Sirloin Steak—A larger steak that is usually between 2 and 3½ inches thick. It is cut from the end of the short loin where it meets the rump (see diagram). Sirloin Tip Steak is just the tip of the bottom of the tenderloin. It is not as tender and usually served braised. Top Sirloin Steak can be tough and is used for London broil.

Chuck Steaks—A steak which comes from the shoulder section. It is not considered a tender cut. It is a cheaper cut that is usually served grilled.

Flank Steak—A steak cut from the shoulder or chuck section of the beef. Each side of beef has only one flank steak. This steak is usually marinated, sliced thinly, or both.

Ribeye Steak—Most people consider this the most flavor-filled steak. They are cut from the rib section of the beef and are typically served without the bone. However, you will see "Bone-In" and "Cowboy Steak"; they are still the same cut of meat.

Hanger Steak—Steak which hangs between the rib cage and loin cage. It is frequently offered on menus because of its flavor. In France and some U.S. restaurant menus this steak is known as "ogle."

Prime Rib—This is not a steak; it is a roast. It can be served with or without ribs, with ribs it is typically prepared with one to seven ribs. The name "Prime" has nothing to do with the grade of beef. This can also be called a rib roast or standing rib roast.

OTHER BEEF CUTS

Brisket—Meat cut in front of the fore shank and is used in corn beef and pot roast.

Short Ribs—Cut from the ends of the rib roast. It has lean meat but lots of fat. Usually served slow cooked or in stew.

Beef Cheeks—Cut from muscles on either side of the cheek bones. These require long slow cooking. They are rich and flavorful. Do not be afraid of beef cheeks because they are delicious.

Steak Tartare—Typically made using tenderloin. Raw, uncooked beef or fish that is cut finely and mixed with onion, garlic, anchovy, olive oil, and egg yolk. It is generally served as an appetizer and eaten on toast or crackers.

Beef Carpaccio (Car-PAH-chee-oh)—A traditional Italian appetizer consisting of raw beef sliced very thin. Served with olive oil and lemon juice; it usually has capers, onions, or both.

VEAL

Veal is a calf, so veal chops, veal cheeks, veal roasts, and veal tenderloin are the same cuts we discussed under the beef and common veal dishes you see on menus.

Veal, as you might expect, is tender, mild, and delicious. However, many people avoid veal because of the abuse to the calves used for veal. Unfortunately, there are people who abuse all types of animals used for food. Let your conscious be your guide; if you feel it might offend your dining companion, do not risk ordering it.

PORK

Mankind has been eating pork for over 9,000 years. Pigs were domesticated before sheep, goats, or cows. Pork is graded differently than beef or lamb. There are three grades of pork: No. 1, No. 2, and No. 3, with No. 1 being the best grade. Most restaurants serve only No. 1 grade. There is also heirloom and specialty pork which is usually better than No. 1 grade. Just for the record, pork has 30% less fat than it did 10 years ago.

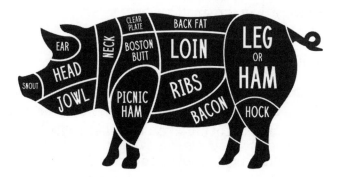

Fat Back—You may see this used to add flavor to dishes or used in a salad. It comes from the pork belly and it has only streaks of meat and is 99% fat.

Scrapple—A Philadelphia treat made like sausage. It is a mixture of meat from the pig's head, corn meal, and sausage meat. It is fried and sometimes served with breakfast.

Ham—Cut from the top of the pork's hind legs. It can be served smoked, boiled, grilled, cured, or roasted.

Pork Tenderloin—The most tender of all pork cuts; it comes from the loin. Medallions cut from the tenderloin are called cutlets. They are usually pounded to make them even more tender.

Pork Belly—This cut comes from the pork's underside. It is boneless and it has a high level of fat. Usually served slow cooked.

Pork Loin—Rarely seen in restaurants, the loin is the area between the shoulder and back legs. It is the leanest, most tender part of the animal, usually served as a roast.

Spareribs—As expected these are taken from the pig's ribs and meat surrounding the bones. These are the largest ribs, but less meaty than the smaller ribs.

Shoulder—This is behind the head and above the front legs. It is usually grilled or barbequed.

Pork Chops—This is from a strip of meat running from hip to shoulder. The bone is usually part of the rib or vertebrae. This is the leanest cut of pork, usually fried, grilled or roasted.

Trotters or Pig's Feet—Slow cooked and usually used for flavor and body in a stock. They can be pickled. There is truly **little meat on pig's feet.**

Rib Chop—Different than a pork chop; it is cut from the lower loin. It is one of the most tender of the pork cuts. The bone attached to these is usually from the baby back ribs.

Pork Butt or Boston Butt—It is not the butt; it comes from the upper part of the shoulder on the front of the pig. It is used mostly for pulled pork and southern barbecue.

Pork Cheeks—Usually used in sausage. Pork jowl and pork cheeks both come from the pork jowl.

Canadian Bacon—It is from the back of the pork and is much leaner that side bacon. It is called Canadian bacon because of its popularity in Canada, where it is known as back bacon.

Charcuterie—A French term for processed meats. This is usually a plate of smoked cured meats and cheese. Primarily, these meats are from pork which is often served on a board. Common Charcuterie meats are salami, capocollo, mortadella, and prosciutto.

LAMB

Hard to believe, but only about 20% of Americans have ever tasted lamb. According to the *Meat Bible*, "it [lamb] represents only about one percent of all meat consumption in the nation."

Lamb is a young sheep under 12 months of age. If it is older, it is mutton or hogget. Lamb is usually domestic, New

Zealand or Australian bred. Oftentimes, American lamb is smaller. Other times, you will see the name of a specific farm where the lamb is raised.

Leg of Lamb—This is just what it says, the leg of the lamb. It is typically roasted and very tender. Lamb lovers serve it at celebrations.

Rack of Lamb—The rib cage of the lamb. You may see it as lamb chops or a whole roasted rack of lamb. This is the most common form of lamb in restaurants.

Baby Lamb—From time to time you may see this on a menu. This lamb is usually less than 2 months old and is flavorful because it has had only milk from its mother, so the meat is milder and more tender.

Spring Lamb—Even rarer on a menu, it refers to milk-fed lamb, usually 3 to 5 months old.

CHICKEN AND FOWL

I doubt an explanation is necessary for chicken; however, because chicken is served in a variety of ways, two species of fowl should be explained.

Capons—These are roosters that have been castrated just like steers. Surprisingly, they are just as tender as regular chicken, and some believe they are more tender.

Poussin—Young chickens that usually weigh less than a pound when harvested. They have very delicate, very tender meat. Poussin is often served in French restaurants.

OTHER FOWL

Cornish Game Hens—An American invention accredited to Therese and Jacque Makowsky, Russian immigrants in the 1940's. When Jacque retired, he raised specialty poultry. After many failed attempts, he succeeded in crossing guinea hens and game cocks. This crossbred had all white meat and was large enough for a single serving. Try it—*you'll love it*!

Turducken—A Louisiana creation that is rarely served in restaurants except at Thanksgiving, but worth mentioning. It is a duck that has been deboned then stuffed inside a deboned chicken, and then stuffed inside a turkey. There is stuffing between each bird.

Duck—Long Island Duck (often labeled as such on a menu) is not a duck from Long Island but is a white Peking. If the menu says duckling, it refers to a young duck usually less than four months old.

Muscovy Duck—Usually a more mature duck. The Muscovy duck is most often used for foie gras. Foie gras has lost its popularity because the duck is force-fed grain (usually corn) until its liver becomes two or three times its normal size. Some states and cities have made foie gras illegal to serve or sell. I never order this at a business meal unless my guest does.

Moulard—Not to be confused with Mallard, this is a crossbred duck between white Peking and Muscovy. If you see "Magrets" on the menu, it refers to this duck's breast, and probably the best for duck breast.

Duck Confit—Usually made from whole duck legs, they are slow cooked in their own fat. Usually they are served with a salad or the meat is shredded and added to other dishes. It is very tender and flavorful.

Mallard—Often confused with Moulard; people have told me that Mallard and Moulard are the same—*they are not the same*! Mallard has a wilder flavor and is smaller than other ducks.

Goose—A richly flavored fowl. It has a reddish, purple meat usually with a hint of gaminess. Geese fall in size between a duck and a turkey. They are usually roasted whole (not in parts).

Guinea Hen—A small bird, originating in Africa, that is domesticated and delicious. The flavor is much richer than

chicken. The hen is more tender than the cock; that is why it is described as "guinea hen."

Quail—A small bird, usually domesticated Japanese quail, that is part of French, Polish, Portuguese, and American cuisine. You may see quail eggs on the menu; they are very small full-flavored eggs from quail.

Pheasant—Native to China, these birds have only been in the U.S. since 1881. They have a wild flavor and typically tougher than other fowl and are commonly served roasted like a chicken.

Woodcock—From time to time I see this on a menu. This is a wading bird; interestingly, their eyes are on the sides of their head so they can see a full 360 degrees. They have stocky bodies, usually have a wild game flavor, and the meat can be tough.

Ostrich—Popular on menus in some places, Ostrich is the world's largest bird. One egg equals about 40 chicken eggs. Unlike other fowl, this is considered red meat; there are even ostrich steaks. It is low in fat and does not appear or taste like other birds.

Squab—A young pigeon that has dark, rich meat. Usually served rare to medium rare, it is common in upscale French restaurants.

Grouse—Heavily built birds, they are similar to a chicken, and can weigh up to 14 pounds. They usually have a wild game flavor and are prepared in the same way as chickens.

Partridge—Medium-sized birds, not native to America. You will rarely see them on a menu in this country. They are larger than quail and smaller than pheasants. They usually have a wild taste.

OTHER MEAT

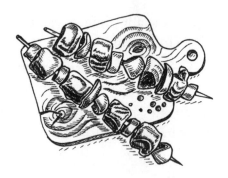

Liver—Calf liver, beef liver, or chicken livers. Liver is often cooked in bacon fat. The calf liver is the sweetest of these meats. Beef liver has a stronger flavor and is harder to chew. Chicken livers are bits of flavor that are usually served breaded and sautéed.

Fois Gras—Liver from a duck or goose. It is the liver from ducks that are fed a special diet that enlarges the liver and makes it sweeter. Goose fois gras is richer than duck fois gras. Both are sliced in various thicknesses and cooked quickly in a hot skillet. It is very rich.

Tongue—Cooked, pickled, or smoked, the steer's beef tongue is most common and can weigh up to 5 pounds. There is also calf's tongue which is more tender and has less fat; it will be on the menu as veal tongue. From time to time, you may see lamb tongue; it is tiny and considered a delicacy.

Sweetbreads—There is a lot of inaccurate information about sweetbreads. The thymus glands and pancreas of the calf are the *real* sweetbreads. If they are beef sweetbreads, they are the same glands and pancreas, only bigger. They are sometimes breaded or served in a cream sauce.

Brains—Commonly this is calf brains. It is the sweetest and most delicate of all brains. It is prepared like sweetbreads sautéed or in a cream sauce. I have also seen them poached and deep fried.

Heart—When I was a kid, my mom cooked beef heart. I never see it on menus, but it is usually calf or beef heart. As you would expect, beef heart has a stronger flavor than calf heart. Heart is a rich meat full of flavor.

Tripe—The stomach lining of the animal, usually beef, which is added to a stew or casserole. From time to time, I see it in French restaurants.

Rabbit—*Very tricky Mr. Rabbit!* You may see rabbit "served three ways" on a menu: roasted, fried (sautéed), and broiled and in a sauce. Rabbit is tender, flavorful, and usually does not have a wild flavor.

Guinea Pig—I dined on guinea pig the first time in Peru where it is considered a delicacy; you may see it on a menu as Cuy. It tastes like pork and is served fried, roasted, and in salads. Guinea pigs originated in the Andes Mountains; they are part of the cava family of rodents. Peruvians consume an estimated 65 million guinea pigs a year. *Wow!*

Venison—Usually domesticated deer, venison, rarely has the toughness of deer in the wild. Much of venison comes from New Zealand. It is usually served as steaks and chops. Some restaurants will tell you the type of deer and the name of the deer farm.

Bison—Maybe you have had a Buffalo burger. This is domestically raised American buffalo served like beef. It has less fat and a full flavor. If not properly prepared, it can be dry.

Kangaroo—A strong-flavored meat; even kangaroo raised in captivity has a strong flavor. It is served like beef and because it is low in fat, it can be tough. "No worries mate," you may enjoy it as an ingredient in stews.

Goat—Also seen on menus as "cabrito." Goat is served like lamb. Kid goat can be very tender and delicious and can be prepared by baking, grilling, frying, or barbecuing.

Antelope—These animals have their origin in Africa. Antelopes are raised domestically for meat and hunting at many farms located in Texas. It is similar to venison but has a stronger flavor.

Elk—One of the largest members of the deer family. Many western states serve elk regularly. Its flavor is not too strong, very flavorful, and is served like beef. I recommend that this meat be served medium rare. The taste is somewhere between beef and venison.

FISH AND SEAFOOD

Anchovies—Mostly a saltwater fish that is a solid, dark fish. Anchovies are small, usually less than 6 inches in length. They taste fishy and are salty. They can be canned, fried, or served as an accompaniment to other dishes.

Bluefish—A saltwater fish with a strong flavor. Many describe bluefish as having a fishy flavor. It has coarse, moist meat with edible skin.

Branzino—A seabass found in the Eastern Atlantic and Mediterranean. It is a large flaky fish, mild in flavor. Branzino is not a freshwater Bass like Striped, Big Mouth or Black Bass. Most of these fish are now farm raised.

Catfish—This fish has moist dense meat. It is firm but not flaky and it has a consistently sweet, mild taste. Catfish served in restaurants is farm raised.

Caviar—Salted roe or eggs of Caspian Sea sturgeon has a rich marine flavor, creamy and salty. There are substitutes for caviar and they all are good. Most would agree other fish roe (eggs) are not as good.

There are 3 popular types of caviar: Beluga, Osetra, and Sevruga. Beluga is the largest and light to dark grey in color. Osetra are golden, medium size, and have a nutty flavor. Sevruga are the smallest and have the creamiest and most intense flavor.

Ceviche—A specific dish, usually shrimp and white fish chopped and marinated in lime juice and enhanced with onions, peppers, or other seasonings.

Cod—May be described as Atlantic Cod or Pacific Cod. It is a saltwater fish with a dense, oily, flaky flavor. Cod is very rich. Many times, it is used in "fish and chips."

Crudo—In Italian "Crudo" means raw. Crudo is a raw fish enhanced with olive oil, salt, fresh herbs, and citrus.

Grouper—A seawater fish that is lean and moist with a mild to medium flavor and has large flakes. It is commonly cut into steaks and sautéed or roasted.

Halibut—A member of the flounder family. Halibut can be an extremely large fish (up to 600 pounds). It is a white flaky fish that is very tender and light.

Herring—A small saltwater fish with a mild, flaky, oily flesh. Herring can be fried, smoked, or pickled.

Mackerel—A saltwater fish in the same family as salmon or tuna. Mackerel has a bold flavor and firm flesh and can be served grilled, smoked, or roasted.

Mahi-Mahi—Also known as Dolphin fish or Dorado, it is a finned saltwater fish that is lean with a mild, sweet flavor and large, moist flakes. The skin is removed before cooking.

Perch—A freshwater game fish commonly served fried or sautéed in butter. It has moist, translucent, white flesh that is firm, flaky, and sweet.

Pike—A long snouted, boney freshwater fish, pike has firm flesh with a rich freshwater fish flavor. In Europe, this fish is considered not good enough for cooking.

Salmon—A series of fish that have a migratory life. Typically, salmon are born in fresh water and migrate to the ocean, then return to fresh water to reproduce. A strange phenomenon is that salmon return to the exact spot they were born to spawn.

Salmon is classified as an oily fish. It has a high protein content. It can be served poached, baked, grilled, and fried. All salmon have a high fat content which makes for a flavorful dish and a great wine pairing with both white and red wine. There are lots of different types of salmon that vary in flavor and texture.

Wild salmon will usually be more flavorful than salmon bred in captivity. Wild salmon that is caught on their way to breeding grounds in fresh water are the best because they have fattened themselves up on different foods in the ocean.

There are six salmon varieties commonly seen in the United States.

- King Salmon (also called Chinook): This is big fish weighing up to 100 lbs. Because of its size, it has a lot of fat.

- Silver Salmon (also called Coho): Perhaps the rarest of salmon, it is only available in the fall. It is firmer, more gamey, and richer than other salmon. Its feeding grounds are the coastal waters of Alaska and British Columbia.

- Red or Sockeye Salmon: This salmon is most often used in tartare or other raw preparations. It literally has a red tone to the flesh (some say orange). By weight, it is the second fattiest, but I think the most flavorful of salmon, perhaps because it lives on plankton.

- Atlantic Salmon (also called Leaper Salmon): Many wildlife experts felt like this salmon was on the verge of extinction. Unlike the other salmon, this one is in the Atlantic versus the Pacific Northwest. It is a fatty, easy to work with, full-flavored fish. Sadly, most restaurants are supplied Atlantic Salmon by fish farms, not from the wild.
- Pink Salmon (also called Humpback or Humpies): This is the most common salmon we see. It is usually canned but can be seen on restaurant menus. It has less fat, so it is a less flavorful fish and relies on its preparation for its flavors. It is the smallest of the Pacific species.
- Chum Salmon (also called Keta Salmon): A Northwest Pacific salmon. When you buy smoked salmon, this is most likely what you will get. It is second in size and may get as large as some King salmon. This salmon is also canned.

Because salmon is so versatile, it can support either red or white wine. Almost all restaurants offer a type of salmon. Another bit of advice about salmon: ask the server if it is "good today." He can tell you because he knows. Armed with this information, you can order salmon off a menu confidently.

Sardines—The name comes from Sardinia where sardines were once plentiful. This saltwater fish is often canned, and the sardine flesh is dense, rich, and oily.

Snapper—There are 113 species of snapper. They are mostly a saltwater fish. Snapper is found around the world in warmer waters. It has a lean, firm texture. The flesh is white, delicate, and mild; often it has a pink tint.

Sole—A flat fish found in the ocean. It is not flounder or Halibut. Dover Sole (a type of sole) is caught off the cliffs of Dover. This fish has small, flaked flesh with a sweet delicate flavor.

Swordfish—A mild tasting, white-fleshed fish with firm meat. Swordfish is usually served as steak. It is a good choice if you traditionally do not like fish.

Trout—A freshwater fish with a mild flavor and a delicate texture. Trout is the most popular of freshwater fish.

Tuna—A saltwater fish with firm flesh and rich in flavor. There are 15 types of tuna. Here are the most popular types of tuna:

- Canned Tuna—There are two main kinds of canned tuna: albacore and skip jack.
- Yellowfin Tuna—Often served raw or in crudo, this fish is firm with a rich flavor.
- Bonito Tuna—A small tuna with very firm flesh and is often served fried. Bonito is considered on the lower end of tuna.
- Bluefin Tuna—The best and largest of the tuna, Bluefin is an endangered fish. It is also known as "toro."

Walleye—A freshwater fish found in Northern America and Canada. It has white flesh that is sweet, succulent, with a mild flavor.

Yellowtail—Also known as Japanese Amberjack, kanpachi, hamache, or buri. Yellowtail is not a tuna. This fish is often served raw or in crudo.

SHELLFISH

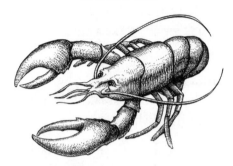

Lobster—Often considered the best of shellfish, you will see lobster served in the shell. This means you do the messy work of getting the meat out of the shell—do not be surprised if you are offered a bib. Lobster served "out of the shell" means the restaurant does the work for you. Clawed lobsters are most often served in the shell, while spiny lobsters have no claws. You will see lobster served in salads, pasta, soup (bisque) and with "surf and turf." The smaller the lobster, the younger it is. Lobster is more tender in the one to two-pound range.

Shrimp—Prawns and shrimp are shellfish; the terms are used interchangeably. There are both saltwater and freshwater shrimp, and they are widespread and abundant. They come in all sizes; tiny to colossal. Here are prawns and shrimp you will see commonly on menus:

- Giant Tiger Prawn—A warm water Asian shrimp used widely in all types of dishes. They have a mild, almost bland flavor.
- Gulf Shrimp— Found in the Gulf and in the Southeast Atlantic, Gulf shrimp can be either brown, white, or pink. White shrimp make up over 25% of Gulf shrimp.
- Rock Shrimp—They have hard shells and a very firm texture, much like lobster.
- Freshwater Prawns—These prawns have a sweeter

flavor and a firm texture. You may see it on the menu as Hawaiian Blue Prawn or Malaysian Prawn.

Shrimp are versatile and are found in dips, soups, pasta, stir fry, and casseroles. Common shrimp dishes include:
- Shrimp Scampi—usually in a garlic, white wine, and butter sauce served over pasta (usually linguini)
- Shrimp and Grits—a flavorful combination of cheese, spices, grits, and shrimp
- Shrimp Tempura—deep fried shrimp in a tempura batter, usually with a dipping sauce
- Shrimp Cocktail—fresh giant shrimp usually served as an appetizer, chilled with cocktail sauce.

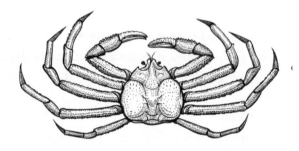

Crab—Crab is a great source of protein, low in fat, and contains Omega-3 polyunsaturated acids that provide protection from heart disease and aids brain development. Strap on a bib because cracking crab is also a messy business.

There are about 850 species of crab. You will not find them all on the menu. Here are the most common crabs:
- Blue Crab—Our most common crab, they are round and a deep-blue green color. When Blue crab sheds their shell, they are caught and served as "soft-shell" crabs, usually fried in a batter.
- Dungeness Crab—A pacific coast crab. It is large

and has a sweet pink flesh. Its name comes from the Washington town of Dungeness because they first popularized this crab.

- King Crab—The largest edible crab which weighs up to 25 pounds. Only males are harvested, and you eat the legs and claws. Its snowy white meat is sweet and delicious.
- Stone Crab—These large crabs are found on the east coast around Florida. They have a season of October 15th through May 15th. The claws are famous for their delicious meat. Interestingly, when they are caught only one claw is harvested and the crab is returned to the water where it will grow a new claw. The meat is firmer than most crab and usually dipped in a sauce.
- Snow Crab—This crab lives on the Atlantic side. It looks like a spider and it is usually served outside the shell. The white, flaky meat is often served as part of a larger dish.
- Peekytoe Crab—This is an Atlantic crab. You may see it on the menu as "Rock Crab" or "Bay Crab."
- Horseshoe Crab—This crab is from our Atlantic coast. They are edible but does not contain much meat. I have never seen them on a menu.

Mussels—A type of shellfish; the most common kind is the Blue mussel found along both the east and west coast. Mussels are chewier and firmer than oysters. They have a mild fish flavor and a natural ocean flavor.

Clams—A type of shellfish from the east coast. The taste is slightly salty, a bit fishy, and often sweet. Clams have a delicate chewy texture and are served both cooked and raw.

Oysters—A type of shellfish found in all seas. There are literally dozens of types of oysters. The smaller ones have more intense flavor than the larger ones. Oysters have flavors of butter, cheese, melon, and salt. They are plump and springy and are served both cooked and raw.

Scallops—These are shellfish that have a creamy white muscle, but they are rarely served in the shell. There are 3 main types: Bay, Sea, and Calico. Sea scallops have a briny flavor and a firm slightly chewy texture. Bay scallops are smaller, sweeter, and more delicate. Calico scallops are less flavorful, exceedingly small and are rarely seen on menus. All scallops can be served raw or cooked.

Octopus and Squid—Both are tentacled sea dwelling animals. The squid has ten tentacles and the octopus has eight. They are usually served sautéed or roasted; they can be served raw or cooked. Their flavor is rather bland and chewy. Many people say octopus and squid taste like chicken.

Popular shellfish dishes you will find on a restaurant menu are ceviche cioppino, clam chowder, shrimp cocktail, lobster bisque, crab soup, sashimi, and sushi.

CHEESE

"Cheese—milk's leap toward immortality." —Clifton Fadiman

Cheese can be served as an appetizer or at the end of the meal. Many restaurants will offer a "cheese course" in which you are offered a choice of cheeses to create your preferred cheese platter; other restaurants have a pre-set cheese course. Cheese courses are usually served with olive oil, honey, nuts, cured meats, fruits, and breads. If you are presented with a choice of cheeses (from a rolling cheese cart or other display) it is good to be familiar with a few basic cheeses.

Cheese is usually made from cow's milk, goat's milk, sheep's milk, or a combination of two or three. All cheese is coagulated milk curds. There are hard cheeses, soft cheeses, blue cheeses, and much more. There are too many cheeses to learn them all; but you will not see American light-yellow cheese on the menu offerings. Here are some popular cheeses: Comté—Made from cow's milk in south central France. Comté is known as the king of cheeses. It is made in large round discs. It has a creamy texture; a nutty, earthy flavor and a long finish.

Burrata—A fresh hard-spun mozzarella made from cow's milk. It has a soft shell wrapped around a creamy center. Burrata will not be offered on a cheese course. It is usually served with salads, bruschetta, pasta, or by itself.

Humboldt Fog—This soft, ripe goat's milk cheese is from Humboldt County in California. It has a distinctive, central line of edible white ash with notes of allspice, licorice, and citrus. It is a great pairing with red wine.

Parmigiano-Reggiano—Italian hard granular cheese produced from cow's milk. Aged 1-3 years this cheese is named for the area of Italy from which it comes. Some think Parmigiano-Reggiano is the same as Parmesan, but they are not the same. "Parmesan" is an imitation of Parmigiano-Reggiano and thus has an inferior taste. Authentic Parmigiano Reggiano has its name imprinted on the rind of the wheel in a repeating pin dot pattern.

Cheese
collection

Parmesan

Brynza   Stilton   Cheddar   Gouda

Maasdam   Blue cheese   Camembert   Radamer   Colby Jack

Swiss   Cheese with spices   Roquefort   Mozzarella   Brie

Camembert—A soft, moist, and creamy cheese made from cow's milk. First made in Camembert, France. it is similar to Brie (from the Brie region of France).

Manchego—A sheep's milk cheese from the La Mancha region of Spain. It is a firm cheese from Manchega sheep and is aged sixty days to 2 years.

Mozzarella—Made from buffalo's milk. It is a soft white cheese traditionally from southern Italy. Rarely offered on a cheese course, it is used in caprese salad and on pizza.

Blue (or Bleu) Cheeses—A general classification of cheese that has cultures of penicillium mold added to the blend. It is usually made with cow's milk (Roquefort is from sheep's milk). The final product has spotted or blue veins throughout the cheese. The most common types are Maytag, Gorgonzola, Stilton, Roquefort, and anything with blue in its name. Blue cheeses are crumbly, with a hint of spice and a rich aroma of lanolin and yeast; most have burnt caramel flavors. You should eat blue cheese last because of its strong flavors.

Epoisses—A cow's milk cheese from the Burgundy region of France. It is a strong flavored cheese that is creamy and chewy with a runny texture. It has a spicy, mushroom, sweet, and salty flavor. Epoisses is not for the weak of heart.

PASTA

There are several types of pasta. Most agree the different pasta shapes and names come from the area of Italy where the pastas are produced. The shapes correspond to the type of sauce that accompanies them. For example, thin sauce for spaghetti and thick sauce for penne. Here are common pastas you should recognize on a menu:

- Spaghetti: Thin ribbons
- Capellini: Thin ribbons but thicker than spaghetti
- Penne: Thin tubes cut at an angle on each end
- Fusilli: Corkscrew shaped
- Linguine: Thin ribbons thicker than spaghetti or capellini
- Fettuccini: The thickest of ribbon pasta

- Stuffed Pastas: Stuffed with vegetables, meat, or cheese
- Ravioli: Square-shaped stuffed pasta
- Raviolini: Little raviolis
- Tortellini: Stuffed shells curved and stuffed in a ring shape
- Tortelloni: Large tortellini
- Agnolotti: A single piece of pasta folded over and sealed to form a rectangle
- Pappardelle: A broad, flat pasta, commonly compared to wide fettuccine

MUSHROOMS AND TRUFFLES

Mushrooms are edible fungus. They have a meaty, earthy flavor. They are grown all over the world and are found in the wild and grown commercially.

The most popular types of mushrooms are chanterelles, cremini, morels, oyster, porcini, and shitake. All have specific shapes and flavors. Portobello mushrooms are among the largest with a deep rich flavor and a meaty texture. Mushrooms are often served as a meat substitute.

Truffles are powerful flavored, earthy mushrooms. There are two main types of truffles: white and black. They have a rich distinct odor and taste earthy, smoky, nutty, oaky, and sweet. The taste varies based on the regions from which they are harvested. Most truffles come from Italy or France. They grow wild and are searched for by "truffle hunters." White truffles are extremely expensive and sold by the ounce.

Now you know what the foodies know, and you can impress everyone with your comprehensive knowledge of food, wine, and dining etiquette. Your self-assurance will impress your boss and partners when you are dining together. When you host a lunch or dinner meeting, your know-how and confidence will influence and sway your prospects and clients. If you are interviewing for a new job or your first job, knowing how to order off an upscale menu and use your silverware properly can help you land the job. If you are training salespeople, you can help them upgrade their social skills, helping them succeed in the business world.

Practice and apply the rules of how to order wine, use appropriate behavior and good manners in business and social settings, and know your way around an upscale menu, and I can guarantee you—you *will* be the "expert" at table.

CHAPTER 14

FOOD TERMS YOU NEED TO KNOW (AKA: READING A FANCY MENU)

You don't need a silver fork to eat good food.

—*Paul Prudhomme*

A delicious meal at a top restaurant should be an enjoyable dining experience; that is, if you are not confused by the menu's food terms, preparation terms, and uncommon ingredients.

Tim Zagat, founder of the Zagat restaurant guide, says that as more chefs seek out high-quality ingredients, the desire to boast is understandable, but misplaced. "If the menu says, 'charbroiled porterhouse steak,' I understand that," explains Zagat. "But if it says, 'porterhouse seared over 5-year-old hickory branches and served with a caramel sauce infused with basil from Tamarack Farm,' that doesn't do much for my dining pleasure."

On the following pages is a basic list of menu terms to help you decipher a trendy menu.

MENU TERMS

A la Plancha	A sandwich pressed and heated using a sandwich iron.
Aceto	Italian term for vinegar.
Aceto Tradizionale	A traditional Italian vinegar.
Agnolotti	A kind of ravioli made with a small round piece of flattened pasta dough, folded over with a meat and/or vegetable stuffing inside.
Agretti	Italian for "agricultural"
Agrodolce	A traditional sweet and sour sauce in Italian cuisine; a term meaning "agro" (sour) and "dolce" (sweet). Made by reducing sour and sweet elements.
Aioli	A sauce made of garlic, olive oil and egg yolk, like mayonnaise.
Antipasto	The Italian equivalent of hors d'oeuvre, meaning food "before the meal."
Arrosto	A dish whose meat component has been roasted or grilled.
Artisanal	Relating to a craftsman, as in a baker that specializes in traditional breads or cheeses.
Assaggi	To taste, try.
Au Gratin	Foods with a browned or crusted top, often made with breadcrumbs or cheese and/or a sauce topping.
Au Jus	Consisting primarily of broth, often used for dipping. "served with natural juices." Pan drippings with the additional broth.
Au Poivre	Prepared or served with a generous amount of coarsely ground black pepper as in steak au poivre.

Baccala Mantecato	Italian dish involving dried cod. Most baccalà dishes require that the fish be soaked numerous times to remove excess saltiness.
Bagna Cauda	An Italian warm dip similar to fondue, where vegetables are dipped before consuming.
Ballotine	Made by stuffing a deboned poultry leg with forcemeat and then poached or braised.
Balsamico	Italian for "balsamic vinegar."
Barolo	An Italian wine, which smells of tar and roses.
Bavaroise	Bavarian cream, originally a French cold dessert of egg custard stiffened with gelatin, mixed with whipped cream, then set in a mold, or used as a filling.
Bearnaise	A derivative of Hollandaise sauce in which shallots, tarragon, pepper, and white wine vinegar are added.
Berbére	A spice mixture which is used in the cuisines of Ethiopia and Eritrea.
Beurre	French for "butter."
Beurre Noisette	Whole butter heated until it turns light brown, giving it a nutty aroma.
Bingham Hill Blue	Raw cow's-milk blue cheese from Colorado.
Bisque	A soup made from shellfish; classic versions are thickened with rice.
Blanquette	A white stew made of white sauce and meat or poultry that is simmered without browning.
Bleu d'Auvergne	Centuries old recipe for blue cheese, creamy but not overpowering.
Blinis	A thin pancake (similar to a crêpe) usually made with buckwheat flour.
Bocconcini di Buffala	Small, semi-soft, white and rindless, unripened mild cheeses made from the milk of water buffaloes. "Bocconcini" refers to the size, uova di mozzarella, (egg-sized).
Boeuf	French for "beef."

Bok Choy	A Chinese leaf vegetable commonly used in Chinese cuisine.
Bolognese	A meat-based sauce that traditionally consists of beef, pancetta, onions, carrots, celery, tomato paste, meat broth, white wine, and (optionally) milk or cream.
Bordelaise	A brown sauce flavored with a reduction of red wine, shallots, pepper and herbs.
Borlotti	An Italian common bean; cranberry bean.
Bottarga	Roe (fish eggs) from grey mullet or tuna, pressed and salted.
Bouchées	Small puff pastry shells often filled with a savory mixture and used as an hors d'oeuvre.
Bouillabaisse	A traditional Provençal fish stew originating from the port city of Marseille.
Bouquetiére	A garnish of carefully cut and arranged vegetables.
Braised	Foods are browned in hot fat, and then cooked in a small amount of liquid.
Brasato	Italian for "braised beef."
Brawn	Also called aspic terrine, made from simmered meats packed into a terrine and covered with aspic.
Bresaola	Air-dried salted beef eye of round that has been aged about 2-3 months. It is lean, has a sweet, musty smell and is tender.
Brie de Meaux	French cheese that is soft, nutty, and buttery with the scent of mushrooms - an AOC[1] authentic Brie.
Brie de Melun	Brie's country cousin, with a longer and chewier aftertaste; the other AOC Brie.
Brillat-Savarin	Cheese that is rich and buttery, triple cream from Normandy, named after Jean Antheleme Brillat Savarin.

1. Appellation d'Origine Contrôlée, or AOC, is a French food-labeling term that protects the style, ingredients, and origin of a product. — https://culturecheesemag.com

Brin d'Amour	"Little bit of love," blend of sheep's and goat's milk rolled in rosemary, juniper berries, and other herbs.
Brioche	A leavened dough with high egg and butter content that gives it a rich and tender crumb. It is called "brioche" because of its shape.
Brochettes	Skewers threaded with meat, poultry, or fish along with vegetables, sometimes served with a dipping sauce.
Bucatini all'Amatriciana	A traditional Italian pasta dish prepared with a sauce with guanciale or pancetta, red chili peppers, and tomatoes.
Budino	Italian for "pudding."
Burrata	A fresh Italian cheese, made from mozzarella and cream.
Cabichou du Poitou	Mild and salty goat's milk cheese with a nutty finish.
Cabrales	Powerful blue cheese from Spain that blends cow's, goat's, and sheep's milk.
Cacciocavallo	In the shape of a screwdriver.
Cacciucco	Italian fish stew consisting of several different types of fish and shellfish cooked in wine, tomatoes, and chili pepper.
Cacio	An Italian cheese.
Calabrese	(1) A region in Italy, (2) or Calabrese. An alternative name for the Italian wine grape Nero d'Avola.
Camellia	Camembert-style goat's milk cheese, clean and creamy.
Camembert de Normandie	A classic cheese from Normandy, creamy and clean when young, sharp and runny when aged.
Canapé	A small, open faced sandwich, held in the fingers and often eaten in one bite, often served during cocktail hours. An hors d'oeuvre.

Cannoli	A Sicilian pastry dessert consisting of tube-shaped shells of fried pastry dough, filled with a sweet, creamy filling usually containing ricotta cheese.
Cantal	A hard cheese that has been made over 2500 years, tastes like a cross between cheddar and parmesan cheese.
Capellini	A very thin variety of Italian pasta that is rod-shaped, thinner than vermicelli.
Capers	Small and round, edible pickled bud of a perennial spiny shrub.
Capon	Surgically castrated male chickens having well flavored meat and soft, smooth skin.
Caponata	A Sicilian eggplant relish made from chopped fried vegetables, seasoned with celery, olives and capers, in a bittersweet sauce.
Capricious Cheese	A dry, hard goat's milk cheese from California.
Carciofi	A Jewish Italian dish of deeply fried artichokes.
Carotte Fondante	Carrot flavored cream confection used as a filling or coating for cakes, pastries, candies or sweets.
Carpaccio	Thin slices of raw meat or fish served with olive oil or sauce.
Cavatelli	Italian for "corkscrew"; used to describe small shell pasta with curved edges that resembles a hot dog bun.
Cave aged Pu-erh Tea	A type of Chinese tea that is classified similarly to fine wines and is very expensive.
Cavolo Nero	Italian for "black cabbage."
Cecily	An Italian herb whose taste slightly resembles anise.
Ceviche	A form of citrus marinated seafood salad, popular in many Latin American countries.
Ceylon	A grouping of curry recipes with the key ingredients being coconut, lemon, and a specific Ceylon curry powder.

Chanterelle	Popular edible mushrooms.
Chaorce	Rich and creamy cheese with a bit of bite at the end.
Chard	A green leafy vegetable that has a slightly bitter taste.
Chartreuse	A French liqueur composed of distilled alcohol flavored with 130 herbal extracts, made by monks within a monastery.
Chayote	An edible plant which belongs to the gourd family Cucurbitaceae along with melons, cucumbers, and squash.
Chermoula	A marinade used in Algerian, Moroccan and Tunisian cooking. It is usually used to flavor fish or seafood, but it can be used on other meats or vegetables.
Chervil	A delicate annual herb related to parsley.
Chianti	Italy's most famous red wine.
Chiboust	Crème Chiboust, also called Crème Saint-Honoré, is a pastry cream lightened with whipped cream or stiffly beaten egg whites.
Chimay Bierre	Rich and pungent cow's milk cheese made by Belgium monks.
Choux Farci	French for "stuffed cabbage."
Chutney	A sweet and sour condiment made of fruits, vegetables, or both.
Cioccolato	Means chocolate in Italian. A bitter chocolate gelato, or any type of chocolate.
Cipolline	A specific type of onion indigenous to a particular area of Italy (Verona).
Citronette	Usually meaning "with acid" or "lemon."
Cockles	1) A grain similar to wheat. 2) A sweet candy, colored white with red stripes originally.
Cod	A fish with a mild flavor, low fat content and a dense white flesh that flakes easily.
Compote	A cooked dish of fresh or dried fruits, simmered in a sugar syrup. Compote can also refer to a game meat dish containing rabbit or pigeon.

Conch	Large saltwater snail or their shell.
Confit	Meat or poultry salted and slowly cooked and preserved in its own fat.
Conserva	To preserve food, as in canned or preserved fruit.
Consummé	Broth which is "clarified" to remove impurities.
Contorni	Italian for "to surround."
Coppa	(1) An Italian cold cut, made from a piece of pork shoulder, dry-cured whole, and is esteemed for its taste. (2) Italian for "cup" or "champagne glass."
Coriander	A spice whose seeds are derived from the cilantro plant, having a sweet, spicy flavor, and strong aroma.
Cotto	An Italian Salami that is cured, fermented, and air-dried.
Coulis	(koo lees) A sauce made from purée of vegetables or fruit. May be served hot or cold.
Coulommiers	"Mini Brie" cheese from France.
Créme Anglaise	A vanilla custard sauce usually used as a topping for desserts.
Créme Chiboust	A pastry cream lightened by folding in Italian meringue.
Crepe	A thin, delicate griddlecake made with a thin egg batter, used in sweet and savory preparations.
Crescenza	A soft-ripened cow's milk cheese with no rind, produced in Lombardy, Piedmont, and Veneto. It is buttery with a rich, slightly tart flavor.
Cresspelle	Similar to a crêpe, a type of very thin cooked pancake usually made from wheat flour.
Croquette	A food that has been bound with a thick sauce and made into small shapes, breaded, and deep-fried.
Crostata	An Italian baked dessert tart, prepared by folding edges of the dough over the top of the fruit filling for a rustic look.

Crottin de Chavignol	Tiny goat's milk cheese.
Crudités	(croo-dee-tays) Raw or blanched vegetables served as an hors d'oeuvre and usually accompanied by a dip.
Crudo	A typical German-Chilean dish similar to a steak tartare. It is made by putting finely chopped raw beef into a piece of pre-sliced white bread and then adding lemon juice, chopped onions and a sauce made of yogurt and mayonnaise.
Crustini	"Little toasts"
Culatello	Italian for prosciutto or ham that is dry-cured and has not been cooked.
Curry	A traditional Indian powder containing at least eight different spices which comprise curry. The word "curry" means "with gravy."
Cutlet	A relatively thin, boneless slice of meat.
Dacquoise	Meringue with the addition of ground nuts.
Daikon	A mild-flavored East Asian giant white radish.
Dashi	Creates the base for miso soups, clear broth soups, and Japanese noodle broths.
Dolci	Literal translation is "sweet." Dolci is used to denote desserts on Italian menus.
Dover Sole	A mild, buttery sweet flavored fish prized for its versatility and for its ease of filleting.
Duchesse Potatoes	A purée of cooked potatoes, butter and egg yolks; can be used to prepare several classical potato dishes.
Durrus	Vegetarian cow's milk cheese from Ireland; slightly smoky.
Émince	A term for finely diced or sliced thinly.
Emulsion	A uniform mixture of two unmixable liquids, such as oil and vinegar. Often used to describe sauces and dressings.
Endive	A bitter leaf vegetable belonging to the daisy family. Endive can be cooked or used raw in salads.

Enoki	Long, thin white mushrooms used in Asian cuisines.
Epoisses de Bourgogne	An extremely rich and pungent cow's cheese from France.
Erbette	Italian for "beet tops."
Escarole	Also known as endive, it is a leaf vegetable belonging to the daisy family which can be cooked or used raw in salads.
Explorateur	A buttery, creamy cheese from France.
Farro	A wheat traditionally found in Italy. It was one of the first crops domesticated in the Near East.
Fennel	A highly aromatic and flavorful herb with culinary and medicinal uses.
Feuillettes	Flaky
Fiddlehead Ferns	Fronds that are eaten as a cooked leaf vegetable.
Fig	Small, soft, pear shaped fruit with a sweet flavor, rich texture, and containing a multitude of seeds. Thought to promote fertility by ancient cultures.
Financier	Sometimes called a "friand," is a type of pastry in French cuisine. The financier is a light tea cake, similar to sponge cake. Financiers are often served topped with whipped cream, berries, or other fruit, and served accompanied by ice cream or other frozen confections.
Finocchiona	A type of Italian salami.
Fiore di Latte	Italian word for "flower" and "coffee."
Fiorito	Italian for "in flower or in bloom."
Flageolet	A light green French shell bean.
Flambé	Food drenched with liquor and ignited.
Fluke	A term for flounder and flatfish that live in ocean waters.
Foglie	Italian for "a piece of."

Foie Gras	(fwah grah) Liver of geese that is fattened using extreme feeding techniques.
Fondant	A sweet, thick opaque sugar paste used for glazing pastries or candies.
Fontina d'Aosta	An Italian cow's milk cheese that must be made from unpasteurized milk from a single milking, with two batches being made per day.
Forcemeat	Ground seasoned meat(s) used for stuffing.
Formaggio	Italian for "cheese."
Fougerus	Brie-style cheese from France that is creamy and decorated with a fern leaf.
Frangipane	A sweet almond and egg filling cooked inside a pastry.
Fregola	A type of pasta similar to Israeli couscous, typically rolled into balls.
Fricassée	(frick-a-see) A white stew in which the meat is not browned but cooked in fat.
Frisée	Also known as Endive, a leaf vegetable belonging to the daisy family. May be cooked or used raw in salads.
Fritti	An Italian fritter.
Fungi	Large group of plants ranging from single-celled organisms to large mushrooms; the most common are molds and yeasts.
Galatine	Made from a forcemeat of game, poultry or pork and usually wrapped in the skin of a bird or animal and poached. Often served cold.
Garganelli	Square egg noodle rolled into a tube.
Garnish	To enhance in appearance by adding a decorative touch.
Gastrique	A syrupy sauce produced by a reduction of vinegar or wine, sugar, and usually fruit. It is often served over meat or seafood to add a fruit flavor to the dish.
Gateau	Various pastry items made with puff pastry and éclair paste; describing a cake.

Gaufrette Potatoes	Thin, fried lattice-cut slices of potatoes.
Gelato	Italian ice cream made from milk and sugar, combined with other flavorings. It is dense and extremely rich and creamy.
Gelée	Referring to Italian ice cream or something frozen.
Genoise	A French sponge cake.
Gianduia	A sweet chocolate containing about 50% hazelnut and almond paste.
Ginger	A fiery and sweet edible rhizome that has hints of lemon and rosemary; fresh and/or ground powder.
Glacé	A glaze used to intensify flavor.
Gnocchi	Italian variety of dumpling, usually made from potato and having a cylindrical shape.
Grana Padano	A very popular semi-fat hard cheese which is cooked and ripened slowly. It is produced by curdling the milk of grass-fed cows.
Granita	A semi-frozen dessert of sugar, water, and flavorings from Sicily, Italy. Related to sorbet and Italian ice, with a crystalline texture.
Gremolata	A traditional accompaniment to the Italian braised veal shank dish Ossobuco alla Milanese. Typically contains garlic, parsley, and grated lemon peel.
Grenobloise	"In the style of Grenoble"" A French preparation of brown butter, capers, parsley, lemon juice and lemon meats with tiny croutons.
Gruyére	Swiss cow's cheese with a smooth texture and a slight hazelnut flavor.
Guajillo	A shrub native to the Southwestern United States that belongs to the Fabaceae (bean family).
Guanciale	A kind of unsmoked Italian bacon prepared with pig's jowl or cheeks.

Halibut	A type of flatfish that lives in both the North Pacific and the North Atlantic oceans and are a highly regarded food fish.
Hamachi	Japanese amberjack or yellowtail fish in the family Carangidae. It is native to the northwest Pacific, from Japan to Hawaii.
Hazelnut	A nut also known as a filbert, often ground and used in cakes and pastries, often accompanied by chocolate.
Hollandaise	A classic French "mother sauce" made with egg yolks, lemon juice, cayenne pepper, butter, and sometimes Tabasco sauce.
Insalata di Mare	A traditional Italian seafood salad.
Insalate	Italian for "salad" or "lettuce."
Julienne	To cut food into small stick-shaped pieces.
Kimchi	A traditional Korean fermented dish made of select vegetables with varied seasonings. It is a common Korean side dish, eaten with rice.
Ladyfinger	Light and sweet sponge cakes roughly shaped like a large, fat finger.
Lagrein	A grape variety native to the valleys of northern Italy, used in red wine.
Lambrusco	A red wine grape. An Italian wine made principally from the Lambrusco grape.
Langoustine	A slim orange-pink lobster found in the north-eastern Atlantic Ocean and North Sea.
Laurel	A plant often referred to as cinnamon.
Leek	Largest member of the onion family. Mild in flavor, and generally served as a side dish. Used in cooking preparations.
Leg Pastilla	North African dish/pie made usually of pigeon, with sweet and salty flavors, crisp layers of phyllo dough, and a layer of toasted and ground almonds, cinnamon, and sugar.
Legumes	(1) French for "vegetables." (2) A large group of vegetables with double-seamed seed pods.

Lentil	A member of the Legume (bean) family.
Limoncello	A lemon liqueur produced in Southern Italy, traditionally served chilled as an after-dinner drink.
Limone	Italian for "lemon."
Lychee	A tropical fruit tree whose inner fruit consists of a layer of sweet, translucent white flesh, with a texture somewhat similar to a grape.
Maccheroni	Italian for "macaroni"" a type of dry pasta.
Mache	A delicate salad green, also known as lamb's lettuce, with a light, nutty flavor.
Mache	A hardy plant whose leaves are used primarily in salads.
Madeira	A fortified wine made in the Madeira Islands of Portugal, which is prized for drinking and cooking.
Maiale	Italian for "pork."
Manchego	A sheep's milk cheese made in Spain, aged for 3 months or longer, is a semi-firm cheese which ranges from mild to sharp, depending on how long it is aged.
Manzo	Italian for "beef."
Marengo	Traditionally, a dish where chicken is fried in olive oil, accompanied with a sauce of tomatoes, garlic, onions, cognac, and crayfish.
Marinati	Italian for "marinade."
Marjoram	A flowering herb that is native to the Mediterranean and has a sweet flavor and strong aroma.
Marsala	A wine produced in the region surrounding the Italian city of Marsala in Sicily; it is fortified much like port.
Mascarpone	A triple-cream cheese used in main dishes as well as desserts.
Mastic	An evergreen shrub or small tree, which is cultivated for its aromatic resin spice on the Greek island of Chios.

Matsutake	The common name for a highly sought mycorrhizal mushroom known to grow in Japan and a handful of other places around the world.
Mignonette	A small, round piece of meat, also known as a medallion; can also describe a vegetable.
Milanese	From the area of Milan, Italy.
Minestra	Italian for "minestrone." Italian soup made with vegetables, beans, and pasta.
Minestrone	Traditional Italian soup made with vegetables, often with the addition of pasta or rice.
Mise en Place	French for "putting in place," refers to preparing and assembling the necessary ingredients and equipment before cooking or baking.
Monkfish	The English name of a number of types of fish in the northwest Atlantic.
Morels	Honeycomb-like edible mushrooms often used in French cooking.
Mousseline	(moose-uh-leen) (1) Sauce or cream that is lightened by folding in cream, (2) delicately flavored combination of white meat, shellfish, or fish and lightened with cream and egg whites.
Mullet	An important food fish for many around the world and can be both fished and farmed.
Muscovado	Unrefined brown sugar with a strong molasses flavor; it is slightly coarser and stickier than most brown sugars, often used in coffee.
Napoletana	Also known as Neapolitan flip coffee pot. A drip brew coffee maker for the stovetop which produces extraordinarily strong coffee.
Nettles	A green flowering plant used in dishes such as cooked greens, soup, or pesto.
Noisettes	A small, usually round portion of meat cut from the rib.
Oolong	A traditional Chinese tea which is similar in taste to green tea.

Orecchiette	A type of pasta native to Apulia, Italy whose shape resembles a small ear.
Osetra	A caviar with a nutty flavor and is prized as an elite caviar.
Paillard	A thin, boneless piece of meat pounded until thin, usually grilled.
Papaya	A fruit whose taste is vaguely similar to pineapple and peach, although much milder without the tartness.
Parmigiano	A traditional Italian hard, fat granular cheese, cooked but not pressed.
Pasta Primavera	An Italian dish that consists of pasta and fresh vegetables. A meat such as chicken, sausage, or shrimp can be added if desired.
Pâté	A spread of finely chopped or pureed seasoned meat.
Pâté Brisée	A dough that produces a very flaky product, often used for pre-baked pie shells.
Pâté en Croute	A pâté baked in pastry dough.
Paupiette	Thin slice of fish or meat, rolled around a filling and fried, baked, or braised in wine or stock.
Pecorino	Hard Italian cheeses made from sheep's milk.
Peking Duck	A famous duck dish from Beijing where meat is eaten with pancakes, spring onions, and hoisin sauce.
Périgord	A former province in France noted for its cuisine related to ducks and geese. It is one of the historically famous truffle areas of France.
Pesce	Italian for "fish."
Pistou	A cold sauce made from cloves of garlic, fresh basil, and olive oil. It is often confused with pesto but is lacking in pine nuts. A traditional garnish for soup (Provençal).
Poisson	French for "fish."
Polenta	A traditional Italian dish made from boiled cornmeal.
Pollo	Italian for "chicken."

Pomes	Tree fruits including apples, pears, and quince.
Ponzu	A citrus-based sauce commonly used in Japanese cuisine. It is very tart in flavor.
Porc	French for "pork."
Porcini	A highly prized edible mushroom.
Port	A sweet fortified wine, usually served with dessert.
Pot de Créme	A French dessert of chilled custard served in ramekins, often made with chocolate.
Poulet	French for "chicken."
Prawn	"Prawn" is loosely used to describe any large shrimp.
Prosciutto	The Italian word for dry-cured ham.
Purée	Food that has been processed by mashing, straining, or chopping to achieve a smooth texture.
Quenelles	Small dumpling-shaped portions of a ground meat mixture, poached (cooked) in stock and often served as a traditional garnish.
Quince	A fruit resembling a large, lumpy pear. Becomes pink and sweet when cooked with sugar and is often found in meat stews and jams.
Quinoa	An ancient grain with a high protein content, beadlike appearance, and delicate flavor.
Radicchio	Italian chicory grown as a leaf vegetable which has a bitter and spicy taste.
Ragout	Literal translation, "To bring back the appetite." A white or brown stew with cooked meat.
Ragù	An Italian term for a meat-based sauce which is traditionally served with pasta.
Rapini	A vegetable also known as rabe, has been described as nutty, bitter, and pungent. A member of the turnip family called broccoli rabe.
Ras el Hanout	A popular blend of herbs and spices that is used across the Middle East and North Africa.

Reduction	A liquid or sauce that has been cooked down to intensify flavors or to create a thicker consistency.
Rhubarb	A vegetable whose stalk is very tart and acidic, requiring large amounts of sugar to acquire the desired sweet-and-sour taste.
Robe	A vegetable, also known as rapine, has been described as having a nutty, bitter, pungent flavor.
Robiola	An Italian soft-ripened cheese with varying proportions of cow's, goat's, and sheep's milk.
Romana	Originating from or referring to Rome, Italy.
Roquefort	An ewe's milk blue cheese from the south of France, considered one of the world's finest blue cheese.
Roux	A combination of equal parts fat, butter, or oil and flour, cooked to form a paste used to thicken soups and sauces.
Saba	(1) The Japanese word for mackerel. (2) A syrup made from grape.
Sabayon	An Italian dessert. An exceptionally light custard which has been whipped to incorporate a large amount of air, traditionally served with fresh figs.
Salame	Cured sausage, fermented and air-dried.
Salmoriglio	A Mediterranean sauce, inherited from Sicilian cuisine consisting of lemon juice, garlic, olive oil, and oregano.
Saltimbocca	A dish made of veal, chicken. or pork, lined or topped with prosciutto and sage; sometimes topped with capers. Means "jump in mouth."
Salumi	Italian meat products which are usually cured and predominantly made from pork. It is equivalent to the French charcuterie.
Sambal	A condiment made from a variety of peppers, used in Indonesia, Malaysia, and Singapore.

Sangiovese	Red wine grape variety originating in Italy; fresh fruity flavors of strawberry and spiciness. Can take on oaky, flavors when aged in barrels.
Star Anise	Also called "Chinese anise," a star-shaped fruit of the Magnolia tree, a bitter, pungent flavor used in many Chinese dishes.
Sassafras	A tree whose young leaves and twigs produce a scent similar to lemons when crushed.
Sauternes	A wine region within the Graves portion of Bordeaux that produces sweet white dessert wine, as well as some dry white wine.
Scafata	Umbrian spring vegetable stew.
Scallopine	An Italian dish preparation where meat (usually veal or chicken) is pounded with a mallet to make it thin and is then cooked.
Scorzonera	An edible plant which is a genus of the sunflower family.
Secondo	Italian for "main course" or "second course."
Semifreddo	Semi-frozen desserts, typically ice cream cakes and semi-frozen custards.
Sformato	The Italian term for a kind of molded custard. It can be a side dish with roast chicken or veal, or it can be served as a main dish.
Sgroppino	Mixed drink with vodka and lemon sorbet.
Shad Roe Borrarga	The edible eggs of a fish from the herring family.
Sherry	A wine from Spain that is fortified with Brandy.
Shimeji	A group of edible mushrooms native to East Asia
Shiso	A Japanese herb that is a member of the mint family.
Sicilian Lifeguard Style Calamari	Calamari prepared with olive oil, capers, pine nuts, currants, and couscous.
Skate	Cartilaginous fish that are carnivorous, feeding mostly on smaller fish and crustaceans.

Soba	A type of thin Japanese noodle made from buckwheat flour.
Sorbetti	Italian for "ice cream" or "sorbet."
Sorrel	An herb that is cultivated as a leaf vegetable. The leaves may be puréed in soups and sauces or added to salads.
Sottosopra	Italian for "upside down."
Soubise	A sauce in which chopped onions and rice cooked in butter are added to a béchamel sauce.
Souffle	A light, fluffy baked dish made with eggs and egg whites, served as a savory main dish or sweetened as a dessert.
Speck	Juniper-flavored prosciutto/Italian ham.
Spiced Belly	Slow-roasted pork belly smothered in a paste of fresh thyme, fennel, and coriander seeds and whose skin is crisp.
Spumante	The Italian term for a sparkling wine.
Squab	Young pigeon meat.
Stricchetti	Italian pasta in the shape of a bowtie.
Sugo Finto	A meatless ragu whose secret is letting it almost burn; the onions begin to caramelize, bringing a special flavor to the sauce.
Sumac	A plant whose dried berries of some species are ground to produce a tangy purple spice.
Sweetbreads	The thymus glands of a calf or lamb.
Syrah Sauce	Also called "Shiraz sauce," made from a grape used in wine.
Tagliata	Grilled beef sliced and served with olive oil and spices.
Tagliatelle	A classic Italian pasta; long, flat ribbons, similar in shape to fettuccine.
Tagliolini	Also known as tagliatelle, the classic pasta that are long, flat ribbons, similar in shape to fettuccine, served with a variety of sauces.

Tamarind	A tropical tree whose fruit pulp is edible and popular. It is used as a spice in both Asian and Latin American cuisines.
Tandoori	Tandoori is a cooking method where food is cooked over a hot charcoal fire.
Tartare	A preparation of finely chopped raw meat or fish, optionally flavored with seasonings and sauces.
Terrina	Italian for "tureen."
Terrine	Also known as paté, a loaf consisting of a variety of ground meats, cooked in an earthenware mold without a crust.
Tobiko	Flying fish roe used to create certain types of sushi, sometimes used as an ingredient in California rolls.
Togarashi	Also known as chili pepper. The part of the plant that is usually harvested is the fruit; botany considers the plant to be a berry shrub.
Tonka Bean	A seed that is black and wrinkled in appearance. It is known mostly for its fragrance reminiscent of vanilla, almonds, and cinnamon.
Torta	A Mexican sandwich served on a sandwich roll hot or cold. Italian restaurants offer Torta as a type of cake.
Tripe	A type of edible offal from the stomachs of various domestic animals.
Trippa	Italian for "tripe," a type of edible offal from the stomachs of various domestic animals.
Trofie	Ligurian pasta made with flour and water, no eggs. It is rolled by hand into little squiggly shapes and served with basil pesto.
Truffle	(1) Rare and flavorful mushrooms/tubers that are considered a delicacy and are quite expensive. (2) Rich chocolate candies that are made with ganache (chocolate and heavy cream).

Tsar Nicoulai	A highly prized caviar.
Tuile	A thin, crisp cookie that is placed over a rounded object (like a rolling pin) while still hot from the oven.
Turbot	A delicately flavored flatfish.
Urchin	Spiny sea creatures that are round and prickly.
Vacherin	Cow's milk cheese that is often eaten like a fondue.
Vegetali Sottaceto	Italian for "pickled vegetables."
Velouté	A smooth, rich ivory-colored sauce generally made with fish or chicken stock, made thick by incorporating a roux.
Vichyssoise	A French-style soup made of puréed leeks, onions, potatoes, cream, and chicken stock. It is traditionally served cold.
Vin Santo	An Italian dessert wine that is very sweet.
Vini Dolce	In Italian, literally translated "sweet wine."
Vini Fortificati	In Italian, literally translated "fortified wine."
Watercress	One of the oldest known leaf vegetables consumed by human beings, having a peppery and tangy flavor.
Yuzu	A citrus fruit originating in East Asia.

ABOUT TOM BLACK

T om's life is the quintessential "rags to riches" story that embodies the American dream of financial success. Tom grew up in poverty; born in the small town of Nickerson, Kansas, the first few years of his life he lived with his family in a railroad boxcar set off the track, divided into two bedrooms with one tiny living space and an outdoor bathroom. Tom did not know that he was poor until, in the seventh grade, kids at school made fun of his clothing. At age 12, Tom knew he wanted a better life.

Tom was the first in his family to attend college. His first year in college he worked for The Southwestern Company who recruits thousands of college students to sell books door to door. With fifty dollars in his pocket, Tom left college during summer break to go to Nashville to learn how to sell on a straight commission basis. He learned the harsh meaning of cold calling: pounding the pavement in the sweltering heat 90 hours a week, going door to door selling books to strangers, encountering homesickness, rejection, and discouragement. Tom watched his fellow sales associates succumb to disappointment and depression, accept failure, and go home empty-handed. But 18-year-old Tom couldn't quit; he was broke, he was hundreds of miles from home; he needed money for food, gas, clothes, rent, and college tuition. He had to make a go of his sales job.

Tom worked relentlessly on overcoming customer objections, the fear of rejection, and the deflating reaction that comes from slammed doors. He worked on changing his sales paradigm; instead of hoping to close a sale every time he knocked on a door, he told himself: *Selling is a process. It's a learning opportunity. Lower your expectations and work on improving your sales skills. Selling is a process of delayed gratification.* Tom made a numbers game out of selling books door to door; he told himself for every ten "no's" he received, he would get one "yes." Tom turned his self-defeating thought patterns into a methodical, motivating, productive plan of action. This was the beginning of Tom's "can-do" selling and business philosophy that helped him break sales records with Southwestern for four straight summers.

Tom graduated from college and he was asked to work full-time as a sales manager for The Southwestern Company. He steadily worked his way up the free enterprise ladder. His teams shattered company team records because of his intuitive and motivating teaching and coaching methods. Thirty years later his techniques are still taught at Southwestern.

Tom became an innovative leader in the banking industry. He was recruited to join Madison Financial, a corporation specializing in retail marketing strategies designed for banks. CUC International soon thereafter absorbed Madison Financial, and CUC then acquired Benefit Consultants. Tom spearheaded the growth of their sales division and under his leadership, sales skyrocketed from $1 million to over $350 million in a matter of a few years.

Tom started Private Business, Inc., a company that pioneered accounts receivable lending for banks. Under his leadership as CEO, Private Business, Inc. grew into the country's leading provider of accounts receivable programs for community banks and their commercial customers. He grew the sales force from non-existent to over a hundred salespeople. The company went public in May 1999.

In 1999, Tom and a partner purchased Bancsource and formed Imagic Corporation as a sister company. Bancsource sells mission-critical banking equipment and ATMs and provides hardware maintenance to banks nationwide. Imagic Corporation provides banks with check-imaging systems. Under Tom's leadership, Bancsource went from an insignificant regional company to a national company serving 4,000 banks in 49 states. Imagic merged with OSI and became a billion-dollar company.

In 2010, Tom cofounded Ncontracts. The company went from no customers to over 1,400 financial institutions, and from no employees to over 200 employees today.

Today Tom is a self-made multi-millionaire. He lives in a prestigious neighborhood in Nashville. He is one of the world's most knowledgeable and well-known wine experts with a wine cellar that at one time contained over 60,000 bottles of fine wine and champagne. Tom counts the world's greatest winemakers, chefs, and wine critics among his closest friends.

Tom is the CEO of Tom Black Center for Excellence, creator of Tom Black's Proven System of Sales Success, renowned international motivational speaker and sales trainer, and author of acclaimed personal growth and sales skills books and DVD training programs. Tom continues to prove his sales systems and business models work.

In Tom's first book *The Boxcar Millionaire*, he shares his proven training methods and sales business models that made him a multi-millionaire. In his newest book *Doing Business at the Table* Tom relates the professional mindset and behavior that gain a prospect's and client's respect and trust, and subsequently, they become loyal, valuable customers. It is Tom's strong belief that with acquired knowledge, passion, hard work, and a can-do attitude, everyone can accomplish their personal, business, and financial dreams.

BOOKS AND DVD SELLING PROGRAMS FROM TOM BLACK

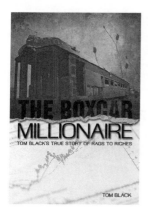

The Boxcar Millionaire

Tom's life is the quintessential "rags to riches" story that embodies the American Dream of financial success. He shares his training methods and proven business models that will help you sell more than you ever thought was possible and achieve genuine sales success.

Quantity Price Breaks available:
6–20 copies, $18.95 ea./20+ copies, $14.95 ea.
Purchase at https:www.tomblack.com/stores
Available in digital and paperback wherever books are sold.

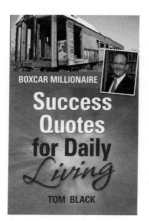

Boxcar Millionaire Success Quotes for Daily Living

Quotes to help you focus on your bigger purpose in business and personal life. The universe will deliver what you ardently believe and act upon. Daily quotes that will inspire, motivate, and help you achieve your dreams.

$19.95
Purchase at https:www.tomblack.com/stores
Available in paperback wherever books are sold.

PROCODE SALES PACKAGES

Tom Black's sales strategies and business models have helped thousands of entrepreneurs, corporations, managers, and sales professionals achieve wealth, professional recognition, and personal achievement. Tom shares his powerful steps of action in his **ProCode Sales Packages** compiled of DVDs, flash-drive videos, and on the YouTube channel.

ProCode Sales Package 1
- Intro to a Professional Sales Career (16 videos)

$49.95

Purchase at https:www.tomblack.com/stores

ProCode Sales Package 2
- Intro to a Professional Sales Career (16 videos)
- Values of Successful Salespeople (20 videos)
- The Approach (7 videos)
- The Perfect Presentation (25 videos)

$299.00

Purchase at https:www.tomblack.com/stores

ProCode Sales Package 3
- Intro to a Professional Sales Career (16 videos)
- Values of Successful Salespeople (20 videos)
- The Approach (7 Videos)
- The Perfect Presentation (25 videos)
- Taking Your Presentation to the Next Level (29 videos)
- Answering Objections (5 videos)
- Inspirational Stories (5 videos)
- Topping Off Your Sales Education (16 videos)

$599.00

Purchase at https:www.tomblack.com/stores

ProCode Sales Complete Video Series (20 hours of instruction)

- Intro to a Professional Sales Career (16 videos)
- Values of Successful Salespeople (20 videos)
- The Approach (7 videos)
- The Perfect Presentation (25 videos)
- Taking Your Presentation to the Next Level (29 videos)
- Answering Objections (5 videos)
- Inspirational Stories (5 videos)
- Topping Off Your Sales Education (16 videos)
- Doing Business at the Table (paperback)
- Boxcar Millionaire on DVD
- Boxcar Millionaire Quote of the Day (paperback)
- Mastering the Art of Success (paperback)
- Success Simplified (paperback)
- Boxcar Millionaire Audiobook
- 12 Month Training DVD
- Foundations for Sales Success DVD
- Foundations for Successful Prospecting DVD
- So You Think You're Not in Sales DVD
- Sell More DVD

$995.00

Purchase at https:www.tomblack.com/stores

For complete details about Tom Black's
ProCode Sales Packages visit:

www.tomblack.com